Building Virtual Teams

T0386326

Exploring the practices developed by remote teams to maintain trust across cultures, this book offers both theoretical and practical resources to enable better working in challenging contexts of project work. This book emphasizes building trust between team members from a practice perspective, meaning patterns of collective, shared activities that are produced and reproduced within the virtual team with the purpose of developing team trust.

The author explores the trust practices that members of remote project teams use to describe their relationships and interactions. Team trust practices are powerful organizational tools for members of remote cross-cultural teams, influencing team decision-making and facilitating team effectiveness. This book offers extensive descriptions of team practices that build and maintain trust in virtual teams in two different cultures: Germany and Singapore. This is a unique contribution as it offers case studies from project teams that were observed and interviewed during their work and provides readers an in-depth, contextual analysis of the trust practices that virtual project teams develop, which previous research has overlooked.

This book will appeal to researchers and graduate students in MBA programs studying project management, human resource management, and strategic leadership. This book is also of direct interest to many practitioners, particularly management consultants and project managers of virtual, cross-cultural, and interdisciplinary project teams.

Catalina Dumitru is an Affiliated Researcher at the Bremen Graduate School for Social Sciences. She has completed her PhD in Business Administration at Jacobs University Bremen, Germany, and her work has been published in the *European Journal of Business and Management Research* and the *International Journal of Management and Applied Research*. Her research interests include trust, project teams, practice theories, and culture.

Routledge Focus on Business and Management

The fields of business and management have grown exponentially as areas of research and education. This growth presents challenges for readers trying to keep up with the latest important insights. *Routledge Focus on Business and Management* presents small books on big topics and how they intersect with the world of business.

Individually, each title in the series provides coverage of a key academic topic, whilst collectively, the series forms a comprehensive collection across the business disciplines.

Trade Governance of the Belt and Road Initiative
Economic Logic, Value Choices, and Institutional Arrangement
Dawei Cheng

The Innovative Business School
Mentoring Today's Leaders for Tomorrow's Global Challenges
Edited by Daphne Halkias, Michael Neubert, Paul W. Thurman, Chris Adendorff and Sameh Abadir

Pop-Up Retail
The Evolution, Application and Future of Ephemeral Stores
Ghalia Boustani

Building Virtual Teams
Trust, Culture, and Remote Working
Catalina Dumitru

For more information about this series, please visit: www.routledge.com/ Routledge-Focus-on-Business-and-Management/book-series/FBM

Building Virtual Teams
Trust, Culture, and Remote Working

Catalina Dumitru

Routledge
Taylor & Francis Group

LONDON AND NEW YORK

First published 2022
by Routledge
2 Park Square, Milton Park, Abingdon, Oxon OX14 4RN

and by Routledge
605 Third Avenue, New York, NY 10158

Routledge is an imprint of the Taylor & Francis Group, an informa business

British Library Cataloguing-in-Publication Data
A catalogue record for this book is available from the British Library

Library of Congress Cataloging-in-Publication Data
A catalog record has been requested for this book

ISBN: 978-0-367-55004-2 (hbk)
ISBN: 978-0-367-55935-9 (pbk)
ISBN: 978-1-003-09578-1 (ebk)

DOI: 10.4324/9781003095781

Typeset in Times New Roman
by codeMantra

To my wonderful children,

Daria and Andrei

Contents

List of illustrations   ix
Acknowledgments   xi

1 Introduction   1
1.1 *Research context and objectives 1*
1.2 *Organization of the book 2*
1.3 *Characteristics and challenges of remote teams 3*
1.4 *Development of remote teams 8*

2 Building and maintaining trust in remote teams   14
2.1 *Defining trust – interpersonal, team, and
organizational trust 14*
2.2 *Integrative model of trust 15*
2.3 *Swift trust model 17*
2.4 *A novel approach: trust as a social practice 20*
    2.4.1 Practice theories in organizational research 20
    2.4.2 A model of building and maintaining trust as
    a practice 23
2.5 *Team case study: building and maintaining trust
in a remote development team 27*

3 Trust and culture in remote project teams   39
3.1 *Defining culture – national, organizational, and
team culture 39*
3.2 *Cultural dimensions theory 41*
3.3 *Trust practices and culture 45*
3.4 *Comparative case studies: trust practices in
Germany and Singapore 47*

4 **Discussion**   59

  4.1 Research summary 59

  4.2 Theoretical contribution 60

  4.3 Practical implications 61

  4.4 Conclusion 62

  Appendix 1 Observation sheet   65
  Appendix 2 Interview guide   67
  Appendix 3 Case studies   69
  Index   71

Illustrations

Figures

1.1 Managing Challenges of Remote Teams by
     Building Trust   5
2.1 Processes of Building and Maintaining Trust   25
3.1 Trust Building and Maintaining Practices in
     Germany and Singapore   48

Boxes

2.1 Establishing rules of communication   29
2.2 Developing a strategy to manage client
     expectations   32
2.3 Adapting the reporting tool   34

Acknowledgments

I wish to thank all the people who supported me in this wonderful and challenging journey. I would like to thank Professor Guido Möllering, Professor Margrit Schreier, and Professor Hwee Hoon Tan for their valuable advice and feedback at different stages of this research project. I would like to thank Andreas Klöpzig and my respondents for sharing their experience and knowledge with me. The empirical case studies would not have been possible without their support. I am grateful to my fellow researchers, Dr. Alexandra Mittelstadt and Dr. Aenne Schoop, for their peer review and suggestions. Thank you to the administrative staff at Jacobs University Bremen and Singapore Management University for providing the infrastructure and support for my research project. A big thank you to my family for their love and encouragement.

1 Introduction

1.1 Research context and objectives

Building and maintaining trust is critical in remote teams from the beginning. This book explores the processes and practices that remote teams develop to build and maintain trust across cultures. Because of the inherent uncertainty and complexity of remote teamwork and the fact that not every team task can be monitored or predicted, successfully accomplishing team tasks and project objectives requires trust. But trust is not effortless or uncomplicated, rather trust must be carefully built and maintained. Building teams on trust heightens well-being and productivity – employees are happy at work and perform well. Trust helps everyone suspend their uncertainty about information, relationships, and complexity, and enables them to relate positively in spite of uncertainty and risk.

Without risk and interdependence trust would not be necessary. Trust is the process of balancing between risk and interdependence in remote teams. But how do team members collectively achieve this balance? What meaning do they give to their interactions? And how are trust interactions maintained and reproduced? The purpose of this book is to answer these questions from a social practice perspective – in terms of patterns of activities that build and maintain trust.

Why remote teams? Risk, uncertainty, and interdependence characterize the complex environment of remote teams, and these aspects are preconditions of trust development and maintenance (Möllering 2006). Remote project teams develop new products, organizational processes, or information systems for internal or external customers, within specific time, quality, and cost constraints (Zolin et al. 2004; Loehr 2015). These characteristics make trust both more relevant and more complicated to achieve.

DOI: 10.4324/9781003095781-1

With this book we want to theoretically explore an alternative conceptualization of trust in remote teams from a practice perspective, and empirically illustrate (1) how trust practices are produced and reproduced in team interactions through the processes of signaling, interpreting, negotiating, and cooperating; and (2) what remote teams do to build and maintain trust (e.g., practices of creating rules of communication, sharing, and rotating power, and checking for common understanding) as well as the cultural preferences and variations mentioned with these practices.

Limited research exists on how virtual teams build and maintain trust in practice, and on the meanings and interpretations that team members and project managers ascribe to trust (Dumitru 2015; Dumitru and Schoop 2016). Much is known about how team members gather and signal trustworthy information but not how they interpret this information in interaction. Researchers usually conceptualize trust in teams as shared beliefs of trustworthiness or collective sets of expectations (Costa, Fulmer, and Anderson 2017), disregarding that trust in teams takes different forms and meanings according to context. Most of the knowledge we have about trust in remote teams comes from quantitative and experimental designs, creating a lack of qualitative field research that could contribute a comprehensive and context-specific view of trust in remote teams (Patton 2002).

With this book we address these research gaps not only by looking at what team members believe, but also by observing how they interact, and most importantly, how they interpret their interactions. What activities do team members engage in to build and maintain trust? And how do they produce and reproduce trust in team interactions? What are their cultural variations and preferences? Answering these questions provides a richer understanding of how remote teams experience trust, and how team interactions produce and reproduce them through different processes and in different cultural contexts.

1.2 Organization of the book

In this chapter we present the goals, the context, and the challenges of remote project teams. We highlight the main research objectives as well as the context of this research: virtual project teams. Why is it challenging for virtual teams to function? What are their distinctive features that make them unique? And how do virtual teams develop?

Chapter 2 reviews the theoretical models adopted to study and measure trust in teams, their assumptions as well as their main drawbacks. In this chapter we introduce an alternative approach of conceptualizing trust in teams as a social practice, including team interactions and organizational embeddedness. The social practice approach offers a complex view of trust by incorporating meaning and interaction through the processes of signaling, interpreting, negotiating, and cooperating. We present an in-depth analysis of how these processes emerge and are perpetuated in three team interactions – establishing rules of communication, developing a strategy to manage client expectations, and adapting the project reporting tool.

In Chapter 3 we present a theoretical overview of cultural dimensions theory, the most widely applied theory in intercultural management and organizational research, and we discuss the relationship between trust and culture. Then we analyze team case studies from Germany and Singapore and explore what virtual teams do to build and maintain trust (e.g., practices of creating rules of communication, sharing and rotating power, checking for common understanding) and the cultural preferences and variations mentioned in these practices. Our findings help us better understand trust practices in cultural contexts.

Chapter 4 offers a summary and a discussion on the theoretical and practical implications of adopting a practice perspective for studying trust in virtual teams. This research also demonstrates the cultural preferences and variations of trust practices and presents implications for designing team interventions and kick-off workshops.

1.3 Characteristics and challenges of remote teams

Remote teams – also known as virtual teams, distributed teams, or geographically dispersed teams – are a dynamic and complex context of organizing characterized by technologically mediated communication (Jarvenpaa, Knoll, and Leidner 1998; Crisp and Jarvenpaa 2013). Researchers define remote teams as "a group of geographically, organizationally and time dispersed workers brought together by information and telecommunication technologies to accomplish one or more organizational tasks" (Powell, Piccoli, and Ives 2004).

Many organizations choose this form of organizing because of the efficiency and the diversity of people from different cultures and professional backgrounds. Transcending time and space with the use of technology, remote teams work across the world and around the clock delivering fast and innovative products and services. The diversity by design of remote teams means collaboration is enabled between different departments, organizational positions, occupations, and cultures. Gibson and Cohen (2003) note that the competitive advantages of remote teams include cost and time efficiency, complexity, innovation, and organizational learning.

Cost efficiency is probably the most important advantage brought to organizations by remote teams. Mediated by technology, remote teams reduce the cost and time it takes to develop and implement products and strategies because team members do many of the tasks concomitantly across time and space without ever meeting in person. For example, for new product development projects establishing a remote team of skilled developers from different parts of the world reduces the cost and time spent on the development cycle.

Complexity refers to the ability of remote teams to solve complex business problems that transcend disciplines, functions, and cultures. By providing the technological structure of bringing together professionals such as scientists and engineers from different parts of the world and with a diverse set of skills, remote project teams allow organizations to develop complex products and services. More innovative and complex products and services result from the interaction of diverse skilled team members within a remote project team.

Innovation is a direct consequence of bringing together team members with diverse skill sets, experiences, and cultural backgrounds. Although this diversity can be difficult to manage for the organization, the increased capacity for creative output outweighs the potential risks. Remote teams embody the positive features of the informal organization because they provide the opportunity for creative expression. Usually characteristic of small companies and start-ups, remote teams become a great environment for aligning the needs of the organization for creativity and new product and strategy development. Additionally remote teams also satisfy the needs of creative, skilled team members to use their ideas and promote collaborative learning.

Performance and organizational learning are direct outcomes of this collaborative endeavor that is going on in remote teams. Much like "a learning community" team members are able to develop new technical, professional, cultural skills, and learn about other disciplines and practice working with colleagues who have a different skill set, working style, and cultural background. This interaction with colleagues from different cultures and departments across the world offers an immense individual and organizational opportunity to develop in multiple areas and topics.

The appeal of remote teams revolves around the ideas of efficiency, diversity, and innovation, namely, that technology enables interaction between people with different knowledge and world views essential for creative and effective team performance.

But the unique characteristics and competitive advantages that make remote teams interesting for organizations also pose challenges. Often the full potential of remote teams is difficult to tap. Empirical evidence demonstrates that the high level of risk and interdependence associated with remote teams can hinder their functioning (Kozlowski and Bell 2003). The challenges that remote teams encounter have to do with their characteristics, i.e., technological complexity, extensive diversity, information ambiguity, and multiple reporting.

We propose that an effective strategy to alleviate the challenges that remote teams face is by building and maintaining trust. Researchers have demonstrated that by increasing predictability and similarity, and managing ambiguity and risk, trust is an organizational resource vital for remote teams. Figure 1.1 offers an overview of the main challenges that remote teams face and the mechanisms by which trust helps to overcome them.

Relying on technology for communication is a specific characteristic of remote teams that distinguish them from other types of teams. *Technological complexity* refers to how remote teams use collaborative technology to work and connect (Gibson and Cohen

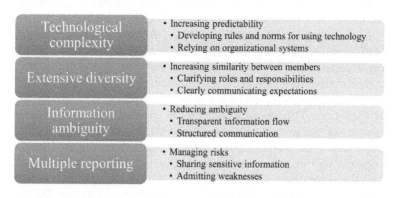

Figure 1.1 Managing Challenges of Remote Teams by Building Trust.

2003). Through technology remote teams bring together specialists from different cultures and regions with a diverse set of skills, enabling organizations to develop complex products and systems. But skills in using technology differ and also the type of technology used differs according to the type of project or task. Remote team members and project managers must therefore develop strategies for dealing with technological complexity.

While organizational tools and technology training are important to manage technological complexity, trust helps team members manage technological complexity by developing norms and increasing predictability in using technology (e.g., how often members should check email, how fast their response time). Remote teams cannot take for granted that every team member is competent in one technology (this must be discussed and established from the start) and also which technology to use for which type of task and project. For example, in new product development projects in the initial phase of the project, ideation and communication tools such as chat and video conferencing are used more while in the execution and implementation phase data storage tools are more necessary.

Extensive diversity refers to the challenges remote teams deal with because of differences between team members who come from different cultures, professional backgrounds, and departments. These differences include personality, culture, language, as well as reward systems. For example, within the same organization, members of the marketing and production departments get rewarded for achieving different results: the marketing department for customer and market development, and the production team for efficient utilization of resources. These different cultures, languages, objectives, and reward systems are sources of communication misunderstandings, team conflicts, and stereotyping (Levi 2010).

Remote teams also experience *time allocation diversity* because team members allocate their time differently as they are usually involved in multiple projects at the same time. Accordingly, it is common that, for example, one team member might designate 30% of their time to the project while another might contribute only 5% of their time. This also depends on the specific point in the development of the project and the task at hand. For example, in the implementation phase of the project the input from the production engineer will be more vital than that of the marketing specialist, and therefore, the production engineer will be required to allocate more of his/her time than his/her colleague from marketing. On the other hand, some team members might assign more time and be more committed to the project and therefore expect and perhaps also challenge the other team members to spend more time on the project. In this way, remote teams must allow for creative ways of organizing their time and devise an integrative approach that takes into account each team member's time constraints.

A strategy to alleviate the potential negative effects of diversity is to build trust in the initial phases of team development in order to promote healthy team functioning (Jarvenpaa, Shaw, and Staples 2004; Crisp and Jarvenpaa 2013). Remote teams that spend time in the beginning of their interaction on getting to know each other, communicating their expectations, and clearly defining their roles and responsibilities are better off than teams who jump directly into the task (Kozlowski and Bell 2003). Trust helps manage this extensive diversity by increasing perceptions of similarity between team members, decreasing stereotypes that pertain to culture and professional roles, and alleviating the effects of social categorization (see Figure 1.1). Social categorization means perceiving team members from other cultures or functions as different and possibly untrustworthy (Williams 2001; Chou et al. 2008). Team members' cultural diversity results in low initial trust at the beginning of the interaction in virtual project teams (Jarvenpaa and Leidner 1998).

Information ambiguity is about managing incomplete and sometimes equivocal information from multiple stakeholders across different communication channels (Gaan 2012). Developing trust helps manage information ambiguity by ensuring a transparent information flow, and developing structured ways of communicating within the team. For example, developing "a single-point of contact" strategy makes for a transparent and structured communication flow. One team member acts as a communication link to his or her work group, clients, and other external stakeholders by keeping them updated with the work progress and soliciting ideas for the project. Each team member becomes the point of contact for that project, filtering and transmitting information from their departments to the stakeholders and back again.

Developing trust between team members is a strategy for reducing information ambiguity in temporary virtual teams (Jarvenpaa, Knoll, and Leidner 1998; Jarvenpaa, Shaw, and Staples 2004). Trust works by ensuring a transparent information flow and developing structured ways of communicating within the team (see Figure 1.1). Information symmetry and good communication are factors that distinguish high performing from underperforming remote teams (Aubert and Kelsey 2003). Good relationships and trust have been found to mitigate the effects of information asymmetry between teams and suppliers (Howorth, Westhead, and Wright 2004).

Multiple reporting relationships is a feature of remote teams that contradicts the organizational single-reporting strategy (Hatch and Yanow 2003). Research evidence shows that remote team members experience a lot of pressure and conflict caused by reporting relationships both to their functional managers and to their project managers and stakeholders. Also, concerns regarding how their performance will be evaluated, whether they will receive any project incentives or bonuses remain unclear for the team members creating ambiguity and uncertainty (Webber 2002). Unclear roles, puzzling expectations, and high demands are factors influencing work overload and competing priorities in remote team structures.

Developing trust in remote teams is a strategy for managing risks (Breuer, Hueffmeier, and Hertel 2016). For instance, the strategy of stakeholder risk analysis offers the opportunity for virtual teams to reflect on their priorities, role conflicts, and performances (Parker 2003). During these team-reflection sessions, team members and project managers can be open about past experiences with the customer, suppliers, and other departments, and share internal, sensitive information that can help team members make sense of the project.

Another important challenge of remote work is the sense of loneliness and alienation that team members experience (Gibson and Cohen 2003). Working across time and space also means that team members rely on technology to meet the social and emotional needs that in a collocated team would have been fulfilled (i.e., security, status, self-esteem, affiliation, power, and goal achievement) (Levi 2010).

For these reasons, remote teams are an interesting context to study trust, because team members work in an uncertain and challenging environment that they must make sense of and manage. Taken together, the characteristics of remote teams lead to several challenges that trust alleviates. Developing trust in remote teams constitutes an important strategy to manage and overcome these challenges (Bishop 1999). In the following we look at how virtual teams develop.

1.4 Development of remote teams

Not only are remote teams complex and diverse in terms of characteristics and processes, but also in how they develop. While all remote project teams are temporary their development is different in terms of composition: some start off and end with the same team members while others have to deal with the inflow of newcomers and even with losing important skilled team members that have a significant impact on the team composition and performance. Organizational changes require teams to restructure and come up with new, dynamic ways of working together. Usually, a remote project team is built anew. Over time, as the project develops, new team members are added to the mix either because of their unique set of skills or because other team members might be required to leave to work on other projects. Although socialization requires more time and energy to be spent at the beginning of the project, research has shown that teams that start off well in the beginning perform better with time (Hackman 1998).

The literature on team-development models is extensive, but our research draws attention to three models that are important for our discussion of trust in remote teams (Gersick 1989; Kozlowski et al. 1999; Marks, Mathieu, and Zaccaro 2001; Kozlowski and Klein 2000). The aim is not to provide an in-depth analysis of these models of team development, but to emphasize that trust is both an essential part of team-development models and a process independent of these models. We acknowledge that team development and trust development are concomitant and interlinked, and we highlight how.

Gersick (1989) observed eight different project teams across their lifespan and surprisingly found that each team had its own distinct pattern of development. However, they all experienced a midpoint crisis in which the teams realized that they only had a limited amount of time to finish the project. At that time team members restructured the way they worked together to complete the task and finish on time. To describe this phenomenon, Gersick borrowed the concept of punctuated equilibrium from natural history and used it to explain how the teams progressed with their work: by alternating between phases of activity inertia and revolution that triggered change of behaviors and goals (Gersick 1989). Her most interesting finding is "that groups use temporal milestones to pace their work and that the event of reaching those milestones pushes groups into transitions" (p. 34). Thus, there is no linear progression in group development but rather there is an external factor – the project deadline – which sets the alarm for the team. Gersick's model applies well to remote teams because they have to manage their activity under time, cost, and diversity constraints.

In their attempt to sketch how temporal factors impact team-work Marks, Mathieu, and Zaccaro (2001) developed their recurring phase model of team processes. In their theoretical paper, the authors propose that teams perform their activities in temporal cycles, episodes that can vary from a couple of minutes (e.g., customer-support teams) to several months (e.g., cross-functional strategy team), depending on the complexity of the task. They further propose that in order to understand how teams work and develop, temporal factors must be taken into account and they differentiate between team processes and emergent states, considering trust in teams as "an emergent state construct that characterizes properties of the team that are typically dynamic in nature and varies as a function of team context, inputs, processes, and outcomes" (Marks, Mathieu, and Zaccaro 2001, p. 357).

Combining previous theories of team development and adding the multilevel organizational theory, Kozlowski, Gully, Nason, and Smith (1999) propose a multilevel temporal theory of team development. This model includes project performance, time, and the organizational influence (e.g., socialization) on team members. Trust is important in the socialization phase of team development, when team members first exchange information and clarify their roles and responsibilities; and in the negotiating phase, when team members must identify and negotiate their roles to achieve their tasks, allowing for a new set of knowledge and skills to emerge at team level and characterizing the way team members interact (Kozlowski et al. 1999). In this view, individual team member attributes and behaviors combine and compile over time emerging as distinct team-level constructs (Kozlowski and Klein 2000).

In all three models of team development the importance of trust is highlighted. Developing effective relationships within the team seems to be just as important if not more important than team members' skills and task performance (Fasto and Larson 2001). In order to build effective relationships, the team must establish and maintain trust throughout its development (Korsgaard, Schweiger, and Sapienza 1995; Fasto and Larson 2001). While the purpose of this research is not to disentangle trust and team development, it is worth noting that trust is an important component of most team development models (Kozlowski and Klein 2000), but more than that, trust is a process.

To conclude, trust is essential for the development of remote teams because through trust technological complexity is managed, similarity between team members increases, information ambiguity is reduced, and risk and reporting relationships are handled. Remote project teams need to spend time in the beginning to get to know each other and build relationships. In order to build effective relationships, the team must establish trust by building and maintaining practices such as offering feedback, communicating expectations, and clarifying roles and goals (Fasto and Larson 2001). In the next chapter, we will explore how remote team members achieve this in work interactions.

References

Aubert, B. A., and B. L. Kelsey. 2003. "Further Understanding of Trust and Performance in Virtual Teams." *Small Group Research* 34 (5): 575–618. https://doi.org/10.1177/1046496403256011.

Bishop, S. K. 1999. "Cross-Functional Project Teams in Functionally Aligned Organizations." *Project Management Journal* 30 (3): 6–12. https://doi.org/10.1086/250095.

Breuer, C., J. Hueffmeier, and G. Hertel. 2016. "Does Trust Matter More in Virtual Teams? A Meta-Analysis of Trust and Team Effectiveness Considering Virtuality and Documentation as Moderators." *Journal of Applied Psychology* 101 (8): 1151–77. https://doi.org/10.1037/apl0000113.

Chou, L.-F., A.-C. Wang, T.-Y. Wang, M.-P. Huang, and B.-S. Cheng. 2008. "Shared Work Values and Team Member Effectiveness: The Mediation of Trustfulness and Trustworthiness." *Human Relations* 61 (12): 1713–42. https://doi.org/10.1177/0018726708098083.

Costa, A. C., C. A. Fulmer, and N. R. Anderson. 2017. "Trust in Work Teams: An Integrative Review, Multilevel Model, and Future Directions." *Journal of Organizational Behavior*: 1–16. https://doi.org/10.1002/job.2213.

Crisp, B. C., and S. L. Jarvenpaa. 2013. "Swift Trust in Global Virtual Teams: Trusting Beliefs and Normative Actions." *Journal of Personnel Psychology* 12 (1): 45–56. https://doi.org/10.1027/1866-5888/a000075.

Dumitru, C. D. 2015. "Predictors of Organizational Trust: The Dynamic Relationship between Organizational Trust, Organizational Identification and Cultural Intelligence." In *International Conference on Marketing and Business Development* 1: 161–67. Bucharest University of Economic Studies Publishing House, Bucharest.

Dumitru, C. D., and M. A. Schoop. 2016. "How Does Trust in Teams, Team Identification, and Organisational Identification Impact Trust in Organisations?" *International Journal of Management and Applied Research* 3 (2): 87–97.

Fasto, F. L., and C. Larson. 2001. *When Teams Work Best*. Thousand Oaks, CA: Sage Publications.

Gaan, N. 2012. "Collaborative Tools and Virtual Team Effectiveness: An Inductively Derived Approach in India's Software Sector." *Decision Sciences* 39 (1): 5–27.

Gersick, C. J. G. 1989. "Marking Time: Predictable Transitions in Task Groups." *Academy of Management Journal* 32 (2): 274–309.

Gibson, C. B., and S. G. Cohen. 2003. *Virtual Teams That Work: Creating Conditions for Virtual Team Effectiveness*. San Francisco, CA: John Wiley & Sons

Hackman, J. R. 1998. "Why Teams Don't Work." *Leader to Leader* 1998 (7): 24–31. https://doi.org/10.1002/ltl.40619980709.

Hatch, M. J., and D. Yanow. 2003. "Organization Theory as an Interpretive Science." In *The Oxford Handbook of Organization Theory*, edited by Christian Knudsen and Haridimos Tsoukas, 1st ed., 63–87. Oxford: Oxford University Press.

Howorth, C., P. Westhead, and M. Wright. 2004. "Buyouts, Information Asymmetry and the Family Management Dyad." *Journal of Business Venturing* 19 (4): 509–34. https://doi.org/10.1016/j.jbusvent.2003.04.002.

Jarvenpaa, S. L., T. R. Shaw, and D. S. Staples. 2004. "Toward Contextualized Theories of Trust: The Role of Trust in Global Virtual Teams." *Information Systems Research* 15 (3): 250–67. https://doi.org/10.1287/isre.1040.0028.

Jarvenpaa, S. L., K. Knoll, and D. E. Leidner. 1998. "Is Anybody out There? Antecedents of Trust in Global Virtual Teams." *Journal of Management Information Systems* 14 (4): 29–64. https://doi.org/10.1080/0742 1222.1998.11518185.

Jarvenpaa, S. L., and D. E. Leidner. 1998. "Communication and Trust in Global Virtual Teams." *Journal of Computer-Mediated Communication* 3 (4). https://doi.org/10.1111/j.1083-6101.1998.tb00080.x.

Korsgaard, M. A., D. M. Schweiger, and H. J. Sapienza. 1995. "Building Commitment, Attachment, and Trust in Strategic Decision-Making Teams: The Role of Procedural Justice." *The Academy of Management Journal* 38 (1): 60–84.

Kozlowski, S. W. J., and B. S. Bell. 2003. "Work Groups and Teams in Organizations." In *Handbook of Psychology (Vol. 12): Industrial and Organizational Psychology*, edited by W. C. Borman, D. R. Ilgen, and R. J. Klimoski, 333–75. New York: Wiley-Blackwell Publishing Ltd.

Kozlowski, S. W. J., and K. J. Klein. 2000. "A Multilevel Approach to Theory and Research in Organizations: Contextual, Temporal, and Emergent Processes." In *Multilevel Theory, Research and Methods in Organizations: Foundations, Extensions, and New Directions*, edited by K. J. Klein and S. W. J. Kozlowski, 1st ed., 3–90. San Francisco, CA: Jossey-Bass.

Kozlowski, S. W., S. M. Gully, E. R. Nason, and E. M. Smith. 1999. "Developing Adaptive Teams: A Theory of Compilation and Performance across Levels and Time." In *The Changing Nature of Performance: Implications for Staffing, Motivation, and Development*, edited by Daniel R. Ilgen and E. D. Pulakos, 240–92. San Francisco, CA: Jossey-Bass.

Levi, D. J. 2010. *Group Dynamics for Teams.* Thousand Oaks, CA: Sage Publications.

Loehr, L. 2015. "Between Silence and Voice: Communicating in Cross-Functional Project Teams." In *Writing and Speaking in the Technology Professions: A Practical Guide: Second Edition*, edited by D. F. Beer, 2nd ed., 351–56. New Jersey: Wiley-IEEE Press. https://doi. org/10.1002/9781119134633.ch59.

Marks, M. A., J. E. Mathieu, and S. J. Zaccaro. 2001. "A Temporally Based Framework and Taxonomy of Team Processes." *Academy of Management Review* 26 (3): 356–76. https://doi.org/10.5465/AMR.2001.4845785.

Möllering, G. 2006. *Trust: Reason, Routine, Reflexivity.* Oxford: Elsevier.

Parker, G. M. 2003. *Cross-Functional Teams: Working with Allies, Enemies, and Other Strangers.* 2nd ed. San Francisco, CA: Jossey-Bass.

Patton, M. Q. 2002. *Qualitative Research and Evaluation Methods.* 3rd ed. Thousand Oaks, CA: Sage Publications.

Powell, A., G. Piccoli, and B. Ives. 2004. "Virtual Teams: A Review of Current Literature and Directions for Future Research." *ACM SIGMIS Database: The DATABASE for Advances in Information Systems* 35 (1): 6–36.

Webber, S. S. 2002. "Leadership and Trust Facilitating Cross-Functional Team Success." *Journal of Management Development* 21 (3): 201–14. https://doi.org/10.1108/02621710210420273.

Williams, M. 2001. "In Whom We Trust: Group Membership as an Affective Context for Trust Development." *Academy of Management Review* 26 (3): 377–96. https://doi.org/10.5465/AMR.2001.4845794.

Zolin, R., P. J. Hinds, R. Fruchter, and R. E. Levitt. 2004. "Interpersonal Trust in Cross-Functional, Geographically Distributed Work: A Longitudinal Study." *Information and Organization* 14 (1): 1–26. https://doi. org/10.1016/j.infoandorg.2003.09.002.

2 Building and maintaining trust in remote teams

2.1 Defining trust – interpersonal, team, and organizational trust

Researchers across different fields and disciplines have defined trust in multiple ways, across research domains as diverse as information systems, political science, economy, sociology, and philosophy (Fulmer and Gelfand 2012). In management and organizational studies there are three main research areas on the topic of trust: trust within organizations (e.g., between employees and management, among co-workers, between and within teams); trust between organizations (e.g., between organizations, their customers, and suppliers); and trust between organizations and the market in which they are embedded (e.g., partner or strategic market alliances) (Dietz and Hartog 2006).

Trust within organizations resides at multiple levels and in different referents; thus, it is important to clarify the focus and the differences between interpersonal trust, team trust, and organizational trust (Costa, Fulmer, and Anderson 2017). Interpersonal trust refers to the dyadic relationship between two team members, or a team member and a project manager. Trust at team and organizational level represents collective constructs developed by the members of the team and of the organization. Team trust and organizational trust can have different referents: co-workers, other teams, managers, and the organization (Fulmer and Gelfand 2012).

In this research we focus on team trust at the team level, i.e. trust about the team as a system of interactions. We are interested in how teams in virtual work environments develop and maintain *trust about the team as a collective unit*. More precisely, we are looking at patterns of interaction and communication in virtual project teams that build and maintain trust – what team members do and

DOI: 10.4324/9781003095781-2

say – relying on each other, taking risks together, speaking out for what they believe in, and admitting mistakes.

To find out how team trust develops and is maintained we analyze the most important theoretical models and discuss what is known and what remains to be explored. According to recent reviews and meta-analyses on trust in virtual teams (Breuer, Hueffmeier, and Hertel 2016; Costa, Fulmer, and Anderson 2017; Hacker et al. 2019; Dumitru and Mittelstadt 2020) the most important conceptualizations of trust are as *a multidimensional psychological construct* based on personal interaction (Mayer, Davis, and Schoorman 1995), and as *a collective set of expectations* stemming from professional roles and organizational rules and routines (Meyerson, Weick, and Kramer 1996). We review both models by looking at the nature of trust, the reasons why team members trust each other and their manager, and the development and maintenance of team trust.

2.2 Integrative model of trust

In this model, trust is a multidimensional psychological construct that develops from frequent interaction, communication, and relationship history. Mayer, Davis, and Schoorman (1995) propose that trust is

> the willingness of a party to be vulnerable to the actions of another party based on the expectation that the other will perform a particular action important to the trustor, irrespective of the ability to monitor or control that other party.
>
> (Mayer, Davis, and Schoorman 1995, p. 712)

This theoretical approach seeks to answer the question of what represent good reasons to trust and argues that team members and managers are more likely to trust other co-workers whom they perceive as trustworthy. Team members look for good reasons to trust, develop a cognitive belief from these reasons, decide to trust and become vulnerable towards the other by acting based upon trust, and expect that the other will act in a positive way towards them and reciprocate.

What is the essence of trust? Trust is conceptualized as a cognitive construct made up of the following five dimensions: positive expectations (ability, benevolence, and integrity), the trust belief, trust decision, trust behavior, and a feedback loop (trust behavior reinforces future trust perceptions) (Dietz and Hartog 2006). Positive expectations refer to the belief that the team member or manager is trustworthy, comprising three indicators of trustworthiness: ability, benevolence, and integrity. Ability or competence means how team members perceive each other's skills in terms of task and job performance; benevolence refers to how team members perceive each other's kindness and concern; and integrity means that team members adhere to certain principles that are accepted or shared by the other party (Mayer, Davis, and Schoorman 1995).

Where does trust come from? Trust develops from the information and knowledge that team members collect from their work environment. The emphasis is on observable behavior, more precisely on how team members gather and interpret information and decide to trust. Indicators of trustworthiness predict future behavior. So, on the one hand, team members decide to trust based on how they perceive the others, and, on the other hand, team members signal their trustworthiness to be perceived by others as trustworthy. Importantly, the process is dynamic as the model contains a feedback loop – information from the environment after the trust has been reciprocated or not changes or reinforces the trust perception.

But everything is in the mind of the team member who trusts – this is a model about how a team member or project manager forms impressions of trustworthiness of others, acts upon them, and then collects new information to adjust their impressions of others. This is their interpretation of the world, and it lives in their mind. In a work environment, team members and managers look for good reasons to trust (ability, benevolence, integrity, liking and being liked by others). Managers and team members build trust by signaling trustworthiness – showing their competency, benevolence, and integrity. Trust is about managing impressions, making sure that within the team there is a belief that team members have the necessary skills (ability), interest in the team's success and motivation (benevolence), and alignment on work values (integrity).

In this model trust is explained as a unidirectional process of gathering information, developing impressions, and making decisions. Trustors look for good reasons to trust in order to make decisions about who is trustworthy and who is not. Contextual information and relationship history are disconsidered, the interaction happens in a vacuum, and there is no information about the organizational factors that influence the decision to trust. With trust there is always a context and a history, there are also other team members that matter, and there is always a meaning and an interpretation of the interaction and the relationship (Lewicki, Tomlinson, and Gillespie 2006).

Also, the assumption is that trustors always have enough information and time to spend on collecting and developing trust impressions. Perceptions of trustworthiness do inform trustors about which indicators people look for to trust others but not how they do this, and a more difficult problem is not gaining information about the other but actually interpreting this information so that it informs a decision (Möllering 2006).

How does trust develop, and how is it maintained? The assumption is that trust develops linearly and predictably. Team members form beliefs about the perceived trustworthiness of others, and these beliefs inform decisions to trust. Decisions lead to risk-taking behavior that then is either reciprocated or not, and this updates the belief about the other (Lewicki, Tomlinson, and Gillespie 2006). Regarding trust maintenance, this model implies that once trust is built it is rather stable because of the feedback loop. Trust is reinforced when the trustee acts according to the impressions they made on the trustor, meaning that much time and energy is needed to maintain trust because team members are always evaluating each other based on their actions. When trust is not reinforced, the relationship deteriorates as breaches of trust happen.

However, this is a model that explains trust development in dyadic relations between team members and project managers where the conditions allow for frequent interaction and communication to happen. The reality of work is that teams often come together in contexts characterized by less frequent interaction, incomplete and ambiguous information, and mediated communication. Team members rarely have the conditions available to develop experience-based trust relationships within the team; therefore, they must build trust differently and rely on other sources. The following model on swift trust expands on this idea.

2.3 Swift trust model

Swift trust refers to trust that is based on roles and surface-level cues rather than personal interaction. Swift or presumptive trust is

> a unique form of collective perception and relating that is capable of managing issues of vulnerability, uncertainty, risk, and expectations.
>
> (Meyerson, Weick, and Kramer 1996, p. 164)

Meyerson, Weick, and Kramer (1996) propose that a temporary team interacts as if trust were present, but then must verify that the team can manage expectations. In a temporary team, team members have not worked together before and do not expect to work together again in the future.

What is the essence of swift trust? This approach argues that trust is a characteristic of the social system, the team or organization, the institution or even society and culture. Trust develops from the taken-for-granted roles, routines and rules of the organizational system. The focus here is on the basis or foundation upon which team members trust each other. We are again looking at what is given, but this time the focus is not on the mind of the trustor and his expectations but on the external world and on the implicit and explicit roles, rules, and routines that are outside of the mind of the trustor. Placing and honoring trust is part of a routine, and team members and project managers trust each other because that is just what they are expected to do. Team members are overwhelmed because there is not enough time or information to develop impressions of trustworthiness, so they look to the organization – What are the rules here? Does the organization support trust?

Where does swift trust come from? Instead of trust being an evidence-driven information process, swift trust is created from category-driven processes (Kramer 1999). Thus, team members confer trust in the absence of personal experience, using membership in categories or groups as a proxy. Team members will transfer or import their trust beliefs onto other members of the same department or organization that they do not know personally and with whom they have no history of working together.

Professional roles and organizational rules and routines are important factors in developing swift trust. Roles provide information about category members, and are both granted and accepted. What is more, they contain information and implicit assumptions about the skills and intentions of that team member. For example, a person in the role of project manager is trustworthy and competent to his team because of his role and his intention to fulfill the demands of this role, and not because of his personality or behavior. Team roles facilitate trust because they reduce uncertainty about the other team members' intentions and competencies. Similarly, rules make team members' behaviors more predictable. Kramer defines rules as "explicit and tacit understandings regarding transaction norms, interactional routines and exchange practices" (Kramer 1999, p. 165), and these rules allow team members to behave in a trustworthy manner, even without direct contact, because one's membership in a team or organization implies an acceptance of the implicit and explicit norms (Wildman et al. 2012).

How does trust develop and is maintained? Research by Meyerson, Weick, and Kramer (1996) on the development of swift trust in temporary groups shows that trust development is a process of updating information about the professional roles and knowledge that comes from the exchange between team members and additional organizational sources, which enables individuals or organizations to trust another without relying on personal experience. While forming trust impressions in this way takes less time and requires less effort, it also tends to be less accurate due to several shortcomings of categorization processes (e.g., bias, stereotyping). Especially in remote teams characterized by cultural and functional diversity, bias and stereotyping are more likely to occur.

In conclusion, the two theoretical approaches offer an important information about the nature of trust and its antecedents but are not enough to explain how trust is built and maintained in virtual project teams because they focus less on team interactions, on what is done and what is said. The models argue that trust develops either from trust impressions developed from interpersonal experiences or from organizational roles and routines that are part of the system. Considerable attention is given to how trust develops – what gets the process going and less on how trust is maintained.

Trust as a practice makes it possible to analyze the pattern and meaning of team activities that build and maintain trust in remote teams (i.e., what team members do and say), and this is important because it offers project managers and team members hands-on tools and information to use in their teams. With the practice approach we are focusing on what team members actively do and say to build and maintain trust. The focus here is on what is actively done – team interaction, team communication, team activities, doings, and sayings. Team trust is built and maintained in practice in what people say and do, it is inscribed in their communication and their social context. Trust always develops and is maintained in a certain context – trust is contextual.

Next, we analyze what constitutes a practice perspective and why practice perspectives are studied in management and organizational studies. Then we describe how the practice perspective can be applied to trust in remote teams, and we propose a model of building and maintaining trust as a practice, emphasizing why scholars and practitioners should pay attention to this approach.

2.4 A novel approach: trust as a social practice

2.4.1 Practice theories in organizational research

Practice approaches started becoming popular in the 1970s and are applied to the analysis of various phenomena such as policy making, culture, consumption, and learning (Schatzki 2005). In management and organization studies practice approaches represent a way of explaining and describing social and organizational processes by conceptualizing the social world in terms of meaningful actions and interactions (Nicolini 2012).

What is particular to practice theory, and how does it differ from other approaches? Traditional and functional perspectives have been dominant in how we explain organizational behavior. In the traditional perspective, organizational behavior stems from the mind and cognition (i.e., psychological, micro processes, agency) of the people who are working in an organization. In the functional perspective, organizational behavior is explained through the influence of the social systems and structures (i.e., the organizational system, macro phenomena, structure) in which it is embedded. But is there a clear cut between micro and macro phenomena? Practice approaches question the distinction between micro and macro phenomena and instead propose that organizational behavior or rather the organizational world is better described as relational networks of meaningful actions and interactions.

Practices are normative – they carry with them meaning about how to act, what to say, what things mean, and what to expect. For example, in traditional and functional perspectives team performance is conceptualized as a product of team members working together towards goals and drawing on their pool of individual and shared resources (Salas et al. 2008). But individual competencies and organizational resources are sometimes not enough for team performance, researchers have demonstrated that teams of experts often fail to become expert teams (Bowers, Pharmer, and Salas 2000). From a practice perspective team performance is no longer just about how team members draw on their shared common skills and competencies and on the resources of the company but rather team performance represents a meaningful pattern of actions and interactions that is socially constructed by team members working within a company and that is being supported and reproduced within the organizational system in which it is embedded. Team performance no longer represents a function of the team members' individual competencies or the resources of the organizational system, but it is the product of the actions and interactions between them. The practice perspective helps us understand why it is possible for individuals to leave teams and team performance to remain the same or why team performance persists even when companies change their team resources.

According to Schatzki (1996, 2002) there are three main components of practices: understandings, rules, and affective structures. Understandings mean the skills and capabilities that inform and help execute the specific actions that compose a practice. Understandings are accompanied by a set of rules, in the form of principles or instructions that direct and determine the course of an activity. Structures of practice refer to a set of ends, projects, tasks, and beliefs that are expressed in doings and sayings that compose the practice. Structures are implicit and normative; when a practice exists, there is a general agreement about how to act in a right way. A pattern of activities becomes a social practice when it displays these three features. Moreover, practices develop over time and space.

With this research, we will delve more into the situational approach seeking to analyze how practices are produced and reproduced in context. Nicolini and Monteiro (2017) emphasize that witnessing scenes of action in their real contexts is vital for studying practices situationally. Scenes of action such as meetings, video conferences, or lunch breaks in an organization are occasions where patterns of actions emerge, collide, and reiterate. By observing these sites, researchers can document how practices are accomplished and how they extend in time, how they are reproduced, and even how practices are disrupted and interrupted.

Advantages of the practice approach include offering an integrative, holistic way of studying organizational processes. Agency and structure are no longer seen as one-sided or independent but rather as complementary and interconnected. Thus, every organizational process is connected to the meaning that individuals are giving to it, to the actions and interactions that are reproducing it, and to the organizational structures in which it is embedded. Organizational processes are conceptualized as meaningful, dynamic, interconnected, and contextual occurrences (Nicolini and Monteiro 2017). The advantage of practice approaches is enabling better and richer descriptions of the organizational world by bringing forth discourse and tools that sustain and connect practices over time (Nicolini and Monteiro 2017). Practices are configurations of actions that carry a specific meaning. To study practices means to describe both the actions that are carried out by team members, and the meaning behind these actions. Practices are more than activities; practices have a pattern, and a meaning of which team members are aware of. For practice researchers the unit of analysis is the activity, the organized sets of doings and sayings meant to reach a certain goal or standard.

Challenges of researching practices situationally include the overwhelming information researchers are exposed to. When observing a scene of action, researchers are exposed to many interactions, projects, and tasks that belong to several practices that are unfolding at the same time. In a corporate office, for example, practices such as newcomer induction trainings, team workshops, and kick-off meetings happen at the same time. For researchers it may be difficult to find out which practices are relevant before starting to study them in detail.

Methodologically, direct observation is the recommended research method to study practices for several reasons. First, practices look quite different when observed in the present than when they are recounted in the past (Warde 2005). Second, practitioners tend to take for granted critical aspects of their work activity such as the basic tasks that they have to do in their everyday work (Schatzki 1997). Third, practices are inscribed in actions and feelings and they are partly unconscious; when people are asked questions about their work they are sometimes unaware of what they are doing (Nicolini 2012). Nicolini and Monteiro (2017) highlight that scenes of actions are occasions where patterns of actions manifest themselves, meet, intersect, collide, and work together more or less successfully. By scrutinizing these sites, researchers can document how practices are actually accomplished, extended in time, and reiterated through doings, sayings, and organizational tools and systems.

So, what is the added value? Why should practitioners be interested in a social practice perspective to analyze organizational processes? Practice theory proposes that researchers and practitioners focus on the meaningful actions and interactions that unfold within the organization. Practice theory encourages us to think more in terms of interconnectedness and flow rather than the duality of agency and structure, individual cognition, and structures of the social system. When we observe organizational activities, interactions, and meanings we gain a much richer and nuanced understanding of organizational phenomena. Practices emphasize the situational, the reiteration, the frequency, and the valence of some activities over others. Studying practices is not just about observing and describing activities but about understanding the meaning, the interpretation, and the context.

2.4.2 *A model of building and maintaining trust as a practice*

The practice perspective focuses on what team members do and say to build and maintain trust and on the meaning of these interactions. Through a practice lens, trust in teams is conceptualized as a social practice – *team members' actions and interactions embedded in an organizational system with the goal of building and maintaining trust.*

A trust practice is *a pattern of collective, meaningful team activities* that unfold in an organizational context and have the purpose of building and maintaining trust. Team members engage in these repetitive activities to develop their work relationships and enhance their performance as a team. Trust practices have a shared, collective meaning that team members co-construct and perpetuate partly unaware. If at the beginning of their work relationship team members are consciously engaging in these activities to build trust, as interactions occur team members maintain trust by perpetuating these practices that over time become taken for granted. Team members perform these activities without actively thinking that they are maintaining trust.

Trust practices are created and collectively shared by team members and characterize the overall pattern of interactions between team members. With time, as relationships develop and activities become more repetitive, trust takes on different meanings and symbols and translates into bundles of meaningful activities. Thus, trust is observed in the bundles of activities that team members create and perpetuate, in their team practices, and in the meaning that they give to these activities. How can we tell if team members trust each other? We can observe how they interact, what they say, and what they do. Understanding the repeated activities, they engage in, offers a richer understanding of team trust.

Trust practices serve different purposes. For instance, in the beginning of their interactions, team activities are more related to building trust (e.g., sharing information, communicating via video conferencing). As team interactions progress, team activities are more related to maintaining the trust. Sometimes a practice can have both building and maintaining purposes, for example, team practices that refer to control or monitoring help team members build and maintain trust. At the beginning of their interactions team members check that everyone understands project tasks, and this shared understanding builds trust. As team interactions progress, a team practice such as regular communication maintains trust. In this research, team practices are complex, and repeated team activities made up of team communication (e.g., the sayings, discourse) and organizational tools and systems (e.g., the communication tools that support these activities).

The unit of analysis is the practice. Rather than analyzing the thoughts and beliefs of team members or the characteristics of the organizational system, we are looking at team activities and the way they are produced and reproduced in interaction. We recognize that team practices are translations of individual beliefs and personality and are embedded in an organization, but we emphasize that they are co-created and reproduced in such a way that they can no longer be traced back to an individual.

Team communication refers to repeated team activities about *what* is being said, the verbal communication happening within the team. Some examples are communicating expectations, clarifying professional rules and procedures, checking for common understanding and alignment, offering feedback on work progress. These team activities build and maintain trust when they predominate over other practices such as withholding information, communicating irregularly and unpredictably, misinterpreting between important and unimportant information, misalignment on tasks and goals.

Organizational tools and systems support team interactions by offering a platform *where* information can be exchanged, a reporting or project management tool to keep track of the work progress, or a team or project budget for planning team activities. How team members use these tools and the meaning they attach to them is what constitute practices of building and maintaining trust.

Conceptualizing trust as a social practice or process is not a new idea. In his chapter on process views of trusting, Möllering (2013) discusses how trust is constantly produced and reproduced by action and interaction. Trust is not an outcome of a process, but rather the process itself "process views of 'trusting' emphasize that trust is always 'in process' and even a process in itself" (Möllering 2013, p. 2). Möllering notes that trusting as a social process comprises, among others, behaviors such as signaling, negotiating, reciprocating, or investigating that help further analyze the development of relationships and the impact that the social environment has on these relationships.

In line with this process view, Wright and Ehnert (2010) consider that people are never in any particular state of trust, but are in a continuous flow of trusting meaning they are always engaging in trust building and maintenance activities. Team members are constantly in a process of trusting by communicating their intentions – signaling, giving meaning – interpreting, and making sense of their interactions – negotiating and cooperating (see Figure 2.1).

In the model above, we present a sequence of the four processes that unfold during the practices of building and maintaining in remote teams. This model offers a prediction of what happens in a team interaction and the particular order of these processes by which trust practices are built and maintained. It is important to note that, unlike other models of trust development that explain

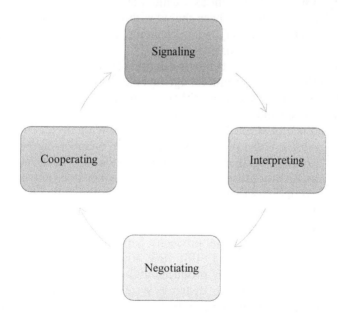

Figure 2.1 Processes of Building and Maintaining Trust.

dyadic interaction, this model is meant to clarify collective trust practices of teams that are enacted by all team members and that are normative in the sense that everyone in the team knows and adheres to these rules and when some members do not act accordingly other members intervene. Thus, we approach the team level, rather than the individual level, and we explain trust practices in terms of discourse and organizational tools and systems that make it possible for trust to emerge in virtual teams through the processes of signaling, interpreting, negotiating, and cooperating.

Signaling refers to the process by which members of a virtual team indicate an aspect that they regard as important for the project and the team. It means bringing forth an important aspect for the team to decide on. Signaling can be done either by a team member or by the manager, the most important thing is that the topic is discussed in a clear and transparent way within the team. Signaling enables building trust because it is a first step to starting the team decision process.

Interpreting is the process by which team members collectively give meaning to the information that has been shared. They reach a common understanding of what is required of them as a team in order to move things forward. Interpretation is about finding out what is important to them as a team, and about making sense of the information that has been shared within the team in such a way that everyone collectively reaches a common understanding of the project, goals, and requirements.

By *negotiating*, team members discuss different aspects of an issue in order to reach a mutual agreement, and satisfy the interests of the team. Team members either negotiate producing a new rule for interaction and working together, or reproduce an already existing organizational rule by adapting it to their team needs.

Cooperating is the process by which team members agree on a way of working together by either adapting the rules or developing new rules or procedures. When a team member does not act according to the rules then the other team members will prompt, and remind the others about what they previously agreed on.

Conceptualizing trust in teams as a social practice that goes beyond the mental and social processes happening at the individual level is a new approach. In this view, trust becomes a routine or practice that is constantly produced and enacted by its members. Remote teams are open, dynamic systems where practices are produced and reproduced in interaction (see Chapter 1). The emphasis in this conceptualization is on the social practices within the team, rather than on the mental processes of team members or the organizational structures that influence these processes (e.g., Costa, Fulmer, and Anderson 2017).

Because previous research has not completely managed to explain how trust emerges within teams, the social practice approach adds an important perspective to the field. By conceptualizing trust in teams as a socially constructed practice, the meaning of this process and what makes it possible for team members to work together can be better understood because we are able to look at the process in a new way. These practices are important because they allow us to understand the network of activities and interactions that characterize the team. When viewed as a practice, trust in virtual teams becomes operationalized through several trusting practices, which are negotiated and enacted, characterizing the system as a whole.

Thus, we approach the team as a social system rather than a sum of dyadic relationships, and we look at predominant patterns of interactions. Interactions consist of discourse and tools that make it possible for trust to emerge in virtual teams through the processes of signaling, interpreting, negotiating, and cooperating. To look at trust practices in remote teams means to explore the network of activities, what and how team members and project managers communicate, and the organizational tools that support this process. This approach allows for a more comprehensive view of trust in teams, that is explained beyond shared beliefs of trustworthiness and collective sets of expectations (Dumitru 2019).

By conceptualizing trust from a practice perspective, we are able to advance our understanding of trust in teams in several ways. This allows us to move beyond shared perceptions of trustworthiness and look at trust holistically by including actions and interactions, as well as organizational tools that enable this practice to emerge. Moreover, when studying trust as a practice, we consider the team as a distinct social entity with configurations of interactions, rather than a sum of dyadic interactions. This adds complexity because we are focusing on how social practices, which characterize the system as a whole, and not just the dyadic interactions within the system, continuously develop and constitute themselves. What activities do team members engage in to produce and reproduce trust in teams? How do they build and maintain trust in teams?

2.5 Team case study: building and maintaining trust in a remote development team

A virtual project team developing a new software in the IT consulting industry was observed, and the data was analyzed with interpretive analysis. The scenes of action observed were the online project kick-off meeting and an online project planning meeting (see Appendix 1 for observation protocol). The project team consisted of seven members working across Germany. All team members worked for over three years for the company and were proficient in company processes. Some had been working in several other remote teams; for others, this was their first experience in a remote team. Some knew each other already, while others had just met there. The project manager did not know them all.

Typical for a remote team, the team meetings and interactions took place online via chat, email, and a video conferencing app, i.e., Microsoft Teams. The project was temporary, with an estimated duration of six months. The remote team's project objective was complex, and to develop, test, and implement a new software for a major client in the hospitality industry. This project involved four departments – one project manager and one assistant project manager, two software developers, two testers, and one sales manager. The main stakeholders were the company stakeholders (project owner, board of directors) and customer stakeholders (project managers, managers of each corresponding department). The estimated project lifecycle comprised five phases: planning, development, testing, implementation, and maintenance.

The main challenges that the project team had to navigate are presented here. Beside the inherent challenges of developing a new product and working remotely, the team had to cope with new software and new ways of working for and with the client. The team had to find solutions to deal with software costs that were too high for client requirements. In the project-planning phase, there were not enough human resources to cover project demands so they had to recruit two new testers. In execution and monitoring, the team expressed their concerns in delivering the software on time and within budget. As the project deadline approached, the remote team started working around several solutions and in the end managed to deliver the product to the client within requirements and on time.

Next we illustrate how trust building and maintaining practices are produced and reproduced in this remote team. When we conceptualize trust as a social practice, building and maintaining trust emerges through the processes of signaling, interpreting, negotiating, and cooperating. In our analysis, the focus is on how building and maintaining trust happens in the social interaction of team members.

To illustrate how our remote team builds and maintains trust, we analyze three team interaction episodes observed: (a) establishing rules of communication, (b) managing client expectations, and (c) adapting the reporting tool. The first team interaction episode illustrates how the team *produces* new rules of communication by changing the organizational practices of writing long emails and developing strategies to manage relevant and irrelevant information. The second example shows how the team discusses and *produces* a new strategy to handle client expectations, and the third interaction illustrates how the team *reproduces* the way reporting is done in the organization by adapting the organizational reporting tool and changing it to fit their functionalities and project requirements. These team interactions demonstrate the processes by which trust is built and maintained (i.e., signaling, interpreting, negotiating, and cooperating).

We chose to analyze these specific interactions because these reflect the patterns of trust production – trust building, and reproduction – trust maintenance. We first present the observation notes and then provide the interpretation. We seek to answer the following questions: How does a virtual team produce and reproduce trust practices? What is the interplay between signaling, interpreting, negotiating, and cooperating? Why is this (inter)action important for building and maintaining trust?

Box 2.1 Establishing rules of communication

1   PM: 'We would need one week to clarify who is doing what. We don't have that

2   time. We are all specialists in our field. We have to rely on each other's expertise,

3   this is the only way we can be flexible and adapt fast.'

4   APM: 'Another aspect about communication is – what is good information and what

5   is not so good information?'

6   M.: 'Oh, yes, please don't send long emails. Here in our company there

7   are so many emails, we can't read them all. They have to be short and to the point.'

8   APM: 'Yes, and then there's the cc issue. I think it's possible to reduce these cc

> **9** communications. *I don't think the project manager wants his email address filled with*
> **10** emails. *A message has a specific recipient; other people don't need to be informed.'*
> **11** T.: *'Maybe it's a good idea to write in the subject if this is just for information (FYI)*
> **12** or if it requires action.'
> **13** V.: *'Oh, yes a very good point: if you really want just to inform specify that it requires*
> **14** no action.'
> **15** M.: *'From our side in support, we really need the number – this is*
> **16** very important to solve the issue.'
> **17** T.: *'What if I don't know it? How am I supposed to know all this information? It's*
> **18** quite a lot.'
> **19** PM: *'Yes, I propose you sit together and discuss the keywords, and then*
> **20** share the information within the team. Now, another thing I want to say that is*
> **21** important in our company is: be hard on facts but kind to people. Please write hello*
> **22** and good-bye, we should respect and be polite to each other. Please always write*
> **23** please – it makes a huge difference.'

After presenting his expectations, the project manager *signals* that the team needs to create and adopt a practice of sharing information. The team *interprets* this action as a call for finding a way to share information efficiently and effectively, and everyone in the team starts engaging in processes of *negotiation* and *cooperation* as they decide how to structure their communication process (how to write emails, who to put in copy, which keywords to use). As this practice is adopted, the project manager asks them to be polite in their emails enabling trust.

The project manager takes the lead and manages the discussion by clearly stating his expectations and those of the organization about how the communication process in the team should work. The project manager emphasizes that there can be no change in the way the project will be documented and reported as he presents his expectations about the team meetings, the manner of corresponding. It is clear that there are certain aspects that will be negotiated and others not, and that this particular aspect of sharing information will require team decision. The administrative, organizational, and communication aspects of the project are non-negotiable, set from the beginning. There is a clear and strong organizational structure on which the team relies which is instrumental for trust building. By clearly communicating his expectations the project manager develops a shared understanding between team members about what is expected of them, and this is a trust-building practice. At the same time, the manager encourages everyone in the team to rely on each other's expertise (L1–3).

When the assistant project manager asks how they can differentiate between relevant and irrelevant information (L4–5), this gets everyone talking and they find out that this aspect of communication is very important to the team and that it reflects the communication within the organization (L6–7). Through *cooperating* and *negotiating*, they develop a standardized, structured way of corresponding via email that focuses only on relevant information (L8–11). In this example, the team members interact based on the assumption that they all know as a team and they can decide which information concerns which function. But in considering this, they are also assuming the risk that information might not be shared to whom it may concern (L17–18). And so they give each other the power and responsibility to act on behalf of the other, assuming they have in mind the mutual interest of the team all the time.

From this team interaction, we observe how signaling, interpreting, and negotiating processes reproduce the structures and resources of the team. Relying on the project manager is an important structure on which trust builds up in this virtual team (L8–9). But the project is so complex in terms of information, knowledge, and decision-making; therefore, team members need to rely also on internal resources to make decisions, and take ownership and control over their tasks, and some parts of the project process. Clearly defining which decisions are the responsibility of the team and which decisions will be made collaboratively by the team members and the project manager will have a positive effect on trust building.

Box 2.2 Developing a strategy to manage client expectations

1 M.: 'They expect transparency in communication. They always say our overhead
2 cost is too high at 4% – they say every other competitor can survive with 1% why can't
3 we? That's what they told us. That's the game and they are playing games with us.'
4 PM: 'Yes, we need a strategy to manage our client – to develop trust while
5 avoiding total transparency. The assembly line is where we can reduce costs and make
6 profit and they don't need to know that. Our strategy is to develop the feeling of
7 transparency without giving it to them.'
8 B.: 'But how do we do that?'
9 M.: 'That's why we're here: to find a way. A strategy, that I know from one
10 of our competitors, is that they have 2 catalogues: one internal and one external,
11 that they share with the client. That could be a possible way.'
12 PM: 'Yes, we need to make them believe that is reality, when in
13 fact it's not.'
14 V.: 'I know [Name of company competitor] is doing that too.'
15 M.: 'Nevertheless, this strategy is tricky and risky. On top of that it means double the
16 work.'
17 T.:'Yes, but we should at least think about it.'
18 M.: 'I don't mean to be impolite, but maybe this could be discussed higher up.'
19 PM: 'Just to wrap it up, I think each person has another priority when it comes to
20 stakeholders. That's a challenge. We can discuss this strategy together with the PO,
21 once we have our priorities in check.'

The sequence of signaling, interpreting, negotiating, and cooperating processes emerges as team members discuss about a strategy to manage client expectations. M., the sales manager *signals* that the client's expectations are unrealistic and that 'they are playing games with us' (L1–4). His interpretation of this is that the client is behaving in a dishonest and unfair way by asking them to cut down their overhead costs. He assumes that the team agrees with him and *interprets* the information in the same way when he says that it is impossible for any competitor to offer such a low cost on personnel. His assumption is right because the other team members signal non-verbally their agreement (L5). This shared understanding is reinforced by the project manager, who immediately agrees with M. and says that they must find a strategy to manage the client by offering the illusion of trust (L4–7). Collective interpretation happens because everyone in the team is acting by having the mutual interest of the team in mind: the project must be profitable for the company while meeting their client's requirements.

The team engages then in processes of *negotiation* and *cooperation* as they discuss possible strategies to manage client requirements: how to have a good relationship with the client, and meet their requirements while ensuring the project remains profitable for their team and their company. Although there are some objections (L8, L15), several team members offer suggestions for implementing this strategy (L9–11, L14, L17). At this point, all agree that this is a strategy worth considering as the project manager suggests to offer the feeling that they are transparent and honest with the client, when in fact the products are much cheaper so that the company can make a profit. This is evidence of maintaining trust because the team members share the implicit understanding that they can adopt a risky strategy and that this sensitive information will not leave the team setting. Even though they do not explicitly ask for a formal agreement at any time during their interaction, there is an implicit understanding of loyalty signaled that all team members will not betray the team by sharing this information outside the team.

M. adds that the strategy presents a lot of risk, that there are a lot of difficulties involved, and this would be perhaps a decision for the management and not for the team to make (L18). The project manager suggests to postpone this decision for later, when they will engage in a project risk-analysis and when the project owner will also be involved (L19–20). At this point it remains unclear which decisions are the responsibility of the team and which should be taken by upper management. Over time, this uncertainty can become problematic and might lead to misinterpretation and possible breaches of trust.

This team interaction shows how signaling, interpreting, and negotiating behaviors produce the structures and resources within the team. Taking ownership builds trust but as we highlighted above it is yet unclear or it remains to be clarified which decisions are the responsibility of the team (which are team decisions and which are the manager's decisions). Clearly defining which decisions are the responsibility of the team and which decisions will be made collaboratively by the team members and the project manager will have a positive effect on the trust-building process.

Box 2.3 Adapting the reporting tool

1 *T.: 'But I don't think it really works for everyone. For another project I sent my*
2 *milestone information and it didn't fit the project milestone.'*
3 *V.: 'We will do it differently then. We still need to get everyone to have an overview.*
4 *We need to have the same understanding. So far we don't.'*
5 *PM: 'First we need to have the input and then we can discuss with the whole team.'*
6 *T.: 'Ok, I agree.'*
7 *M.: 'This project tool is created specifically for our company. There is some flexibility*
8 *and room for discussion… but it cannot all be planned in really all the details but in*
9 *overall milestones set by the client.'*
10 *B.: 'But how was this tool developed and how were these work packages*
11 *designed? They don't make any sense!'*
12 *PM: 'They were developed based on information from workshops with people from*
13 *all across our company's departments.'*
14 *T.: 'But the information in the software is too general. What we do is much more*
15 *complex than that.'*
16 *V.: 'What I can suggest is that if you want to change*
17 *something you contact me. We will make it work, we have your back.'*

T. *signals* several weaknesses in the project management tool that the organization has recently implemented (L1–2). In response to T., V. *interprets* his suggestion as a proposition to change the structure of the reporting tool and for that matter he assumes everyone in the team agrees to do it differently, but then he emphasizes that in order to do that they need to have a shared understanding of the project (L3–4). A shared understanding still needs to be reached, but there is a good basis on which the interaction starts. The project manager agrees to this when he adds that the team still needs additional information (L5). T. also agrees (L6), while M. adds information about the structure and purpose of the organizational tool (L7–9). B. gives his own candid *interpretation* and addresses a key weakness of the project management tool – the lack of specificity in the work packages (L10–11). T. agrees with him, while the project manager and T. start *negotiating* and *cooperating* by highlighting that the tool can be adapted to fit their team and project requirements (L12–15). V. adds that they will support each other if they have any changes that they want to make to the project tool, and change the structure (L16–17).

These interactions demonstrate how processes of signaling, interpreting, negotiating, and cooperating work to maintain trust. Team members already trust each other enough, so there is a strong basis upon which to provide a good flow of information and to communicate in order to work on the already existing reporting tool. This consists of a bottom-up approach because a team member signals that the reporting tool needs to be changed and adapted in order to fit the requirements of the project. And so the team agrees that this will be done. What is addressed from the beginning by team members is immediately supported by the manager. The project manager had previously stated: "You are the specialists, you know what the best option is. We have to trust each other." The meaning behind this is that, on the one hand, team members are empowered to take responsibility and make decisions, and, on the other hand, to speak up and voice their concerns whichever these may be. Speaking up and voicing concerns act as maintaining trust because meaning is perpetuated within the team.

This team interaction shows how signaling, interpreting, negotiating, and cooperating reproduce the organizational structures and resources. The project reporting system is an organizational tool designed to help team members and managers plan, organize, and monitor their projects. But just as with any organizational value or tool, the team does not merely import it but it must adapt it to their own needs. This adaptation and sense-making results in building trust.

In these team interactions, we observed *how* trust as a practice emerges in virtual teams and we analyzed how team members establish rules of communication, make a tentative to develop a strategy to manage client expectations, and adapt the project management tool. We have structured this analysis by addressing four processes through which trust emerges signaling, interpreting, negotiating, and cooperating. These interactions matter because they demonstrate how trust as a social practice emerges through the production and reproduction of rules and structures.

In the next chapter we add another level of complexity as we explore how virtual teams in Germany and Singapore use trust practices. We analyze interviews with virtual teams from Germany and Singapore and learn (1) how virtual teams describe practices that build and sustain trust and (2) how differences in cultural values explain why some trust practices are more frequently described than others.

References

Bowers, C. A., J. A. Pharmer, and E. Salas. 2000. "When Member Homogeneity Is Needed in Work Teams: A Meta-Analysis." *Small Group Research* 31 (3): 305–27. https://doi.org/10.1177/104649640003100303.

Breuer, C., J. Hueffmeier, and G. Hertel. 2016. "Does Trust Matter More in Virtual Teams? A Meta-Analysis of Trust and Team Effectiveness Considering Virtuality and Documentation as Moderators." *Journal of Applied Psychology* 101 (8): 1151–77. https://doi.org/10.1037/apl0000113.

Costa, A. C., C. A. Fulmer, and N. R. Anderson. 2017. "Trust in Work Teams: An Integrative Review, Multilevel Model, and Future Directions." *Journal of Organizational Behavior*: 1–16. https://doi.org/10.1002/job.2213.

Dietz, G., and D. N. Den Hartog. 2006. "Measuring Trust inside Organisations." *Personnel Review* 35 (5): 557–88. https://doi.org/10.1108/0048 3480610682299.

Dumitru, C. D. 2019. "Practices of Building and Maintaining Trust in Cross-Functional Teams." Information Resource Center der Jacobs University Bremen. https://opus.jacobs-university.de/frontdoor/index/index/docId/886

Dumitru, C. D., and A. Mittelstadt. 2020. "What We Know and What We Do Not Know about Trust in Work Teams: A Systematic Literature Review." *European Journal of Business and Management Research* 5 (3): 1–11. https://doi.org/10.24018/ejbmr.2020.5.3.303.

Fulmer, C. A., and M. J. Gelfand. 2012. "At What Level (and in Whom) We Trust: Trust across Multiple Organizational Levels." *Journal of Management* 38 (4): 1167–1230. https://doi.org/10.1177/0149206312439327.

Hacker, J., M. Johnson, C. Saunders, and A. L. Thayer. 2019. "Trust in Virtual Teams: A Multidisciplinary Review and Integration." *Australasian Journal of Information Systems* 23 (1): 1–36. *Information Systems* 14 (4): 29–64. https://doi.org/10.1080/07421222.1998.1 1518185.

Kramer, R. M. 1999. "Trust and Distrust in Organizations: Emerging Perspectives, Enduring Questions." *Annual Review of Psychology* 50 (January): 569–98. https://doi.org/10.1146/annurev.psych.50.1.569.

Lewicki, R. J., E. C. Tomlinson, and N. Gillespie. 2006. "Models of Interpersonal Trust Development: Theoretical Approaches, Empirical Evidence, and Future Directions." *Journal of Management* 32 (6): 991–1022. https://doi.org/10.1177/0149206306294405.

Mayer, R. C., J. H. Davis, and F. D. Schoorman. 1995. "An Integrative Model of Organizational Trust." *The Academy of Management Review* 20 (3): 709–34.

Meyerson, D., K. E. Weick, and R. M. Kramer. 1996. "Swift Trust and Temporary Groups." In *Trust in Organizations: Frontiers of Theory and Research*, edited by R. M. Kramer and T. R. Tyler, 1st ed., 166–95. Thousand Oaks, CA: Sage Publications.

Möllering, Guido. 2006. *Trust: Reason, Routine, Reflexivity.* Oxford: Elsevier.

———. 2013. "Process Views of Trusting and Crises." In *Handbook of Advances in Trust Research*, edited by Reinhard Bachmann and Akbar Zaheer, 1–18. Cheltenham: Edward Elgar Publishing.

Nicolini, D. 2012. *Practice Theory, Work, and Organization: An Introduction.* 1st ed. Oxford: Oxford University Press.

Nicolini, D., and P. Monteiro. 2017. "The Practice Approach: For a Praxeology of Organisational and Management Studies." In *The SAGE Handbook of Process Organization Studies*, edited by A. Langley and H. Tsoukas, 1st ed., 1–27. London: Sage Publications. https://doi.org/10.4135/9781473957954.n7.

Salas, E., D. Diazgranados, C. Klein, C. S. Burke, C. Kevin, C. Florida, G. F. Goodwin, and S. M. Halpin. 2008. "Does Team Training Improve Team Performance? A Meta-Analysis." *Human Factors* 50 (6): 903–33. https://doi.org/10.1518/001872008X375009.

Schatzki, T. R. March. 2005. "Peripheral Vision: The Sites of Organizations." *Organization Studies* 26(3): 465–84. https://doi.org/10.1177/01 70840605050876.

Schatzki, T. R. 1997. "Practices and Actions: A Wittgensteinian Critique of Bourdieu and Giddens." *Philosophy of the Social Sciences* 27 (3): 283–308. https://doi.org/10.1177/004839319702700301.

Warde, A. 2005. "Consumption and Theories of Practice." *Journal of Consumer Culture* 5 (2): 131–53. https://doi.org/10.1177/1469540505053090.

Wildman, J. L., M. L. Shuffler, E. H. Lazzara, S. M. Fiore, C. S. Burke, E. Salas, and S. Garven. 2012. "Trust Development in Swift Starting Action Teams: A Multilevel Framework." *Group & Organization Management* 37: 137–70. https://doi.org/10.1177/1059601111434202.

Wright, A., and I. Ehnert. 2010. "Making Sense of Trust across Cultural Contexts." In *Organizational Trust: A Cultural Perspective*, edited by M. N. K. Saunders, D. Skinner, G. Dietz, N. Gillespie, and R. J. Lewicki, 1st ed., 107–26. New York: Cambridge University Press. https://doi.org/10.1017/CBO9780511763106.005.

3 Trust and culture in remote project teams

3.1 Defining culture – national, organizational, and team culture

There are many approaches to examining culture. Some researchers define culture as an internalized and shared set of assumptions, expectations, procedures, and ways of doing things that have been internalized to the extent that they become taken for granted (Triandis 1972). Other definitions focus on culture as a part of who we are, of our identity that creates a sense of belonging or not belonging "the collective programming of the mind which distinguishes one group (nation, society) from another" (Hofstede 2001).

The study of human culture and the differences between cultures are core research topics of anthropology. The central questions that anthropologists ask about culture is how universal human culture is and how we can study it. Anthropological research on the topic of human culture introduced the concept of cultural relativism which means that there is not one universal human culture but many different ones, each unique and valid in its own context (Geertz 1973).

From anthropology, culture was introduced in management and organizational studies research with the famous, paradigm-shifting Hofstede study of a multinational company across 70 countries (Hofstede 1980, 2001). Since then, research in intercultural management has grown exponentially (Chanlat 2012). There are three approaches that dominate the discussion on cross-cultural management and work: convergence, hybridization, and divergence (Chanlat 2017). In the convergent approach national cultures are becoming increasingly global and have the tendency to gravitate towards similar work values, regardless of nation or region. Hybridization emphasizes the idea that as interaction between cultures becomes increasingly frequent, the result is a new blended work culture. The divergent approach is the one most often represented

DOI: 10.4324/9781003095781-3

in management research, and it addresses the specificity of culture and emphasizes that differences will always exist when people from different countries work together.

There are different types and levels of culture: national, organizational, and team. National culture refers to the set of values and beliefs shared by people living in the same geographic place, sharing the same language, history, and customs. Organizational culture means the system of values upon which an organization is formed; it contains the vision of the organization, and its role is to guide employees and make them feel part of a company. Team culture refers to a subculture within the organization; it can be a project team, a department, or a business unit. For example, within the same company the accounting department team may have a subculture that emphasizes different values than a research and development department or a marketing department. People can be part of and identify with several subcultures from the organization a person works for to the fitness club that person belongs to.

The building blocks of culture are values (Schein 2010). Values are beliefs that transcend situations, guide behavior and events, and serve both individual and collective interests (Schwartz 2012). For example, people will adhere to values such as power, achievement, and self-direction that serve their individual interests while simultaneously adhering to values such as benevolence, tradition, and conformity that serve group interest (Schwartz 2012). Cultural values are not given but acquired, and learned through language, stories, beliefs, and norms developed over a lifetime. In our global work life, we often interact with people from different cultures and these interactions offer valuable lessons on how cultural traditions and beliefs influence the way people work together and build trust.

In this research, our goal is to explore variations and preferences in trust practices in virtual teams in Germany and Singapore; we therefore consider nationality a proxy for culture. In doing so we assume that virtual team members and managers have different work values because they have been socialized in different geographical areas, speak different languages, and have different approaches to teamwork. We acknowledge that other factors might also influence their trust building and maintaining practices such as organizational practices, communication styles, and work experience (Staples and Zhao 2006), but our research will zoom in on cultural preferences and variations.

Cultural dimensions theory is the theory that helps us better understand cultural differences and the relationship with trust.

3.2 Cultural dimensions theory

Hofstede proposed a framework for understanding culture in organizations setting out to empirically verify, anthropologists Kroeber and Kluckhohn (1952) claim, that cultures are divided into universal categories that all respond to the same existential human questions. While the questions they describe are universal, how a society responds to these questions differs across cultures. Each dimension is "rooted in a basic problem with which all societies have to cope, but on which their answers vary" (Hofstede, Hofstede, and Minkov 2010).

Culture is a set of shared socialization skills specific to people who have grown up in the same society. Every person carries certain modes of thinking, acting, and feeling, developed during childhood and often shared among the people in a group. Through the cultural group and reciprocity of the shared values, these values become part of each individual. Hofstede calls this the mental software of a cultural group.

When studying organizational processes in a global company Hofstede had access to a large amount of data and was able to demonstrate how national culture impacted on several organizational processes and find consistent patterns of how different nationalities differ on several dimensions. Over the next 25 years, Hofstede analyzed these patterns in other organizations and in other countries and identified six independent dimensions of national culture. "A dimension is an aspect of a culture that can be measured relative to other cultures." (Hofstede 2011).

Initially Hofstede identified four dimensions. As he continued his work and collaborations, further dimensions were added. In the 1980s, based on Bond's work with the Chinese Value Survey, a fifth dimension long-term/short-term orientation was added (Hofstede and Bond 1988). In the 2000s, based on Minkov's work, a sixth-dimension indulgence/restraint was added (Hofstede, Hofstede, and Minkov 2010). The six dimensions are as follows: power distance (solution to human inequality), uncertainty avoidance (related to stress about the unknown future), individualism/collectivism (group integration), masculinity/femininity (emotional role division), long-term/short-term orientation (choice of focus: future or present and past), and indulgence/restraint (gratification or control of desires to enjoy life). Next, we discuss each cultural dimension.

Power distance expresses the attitude towards inequality. Power distance is about how people who have less power expect and accept that power is not distributed equally. Low-power distance countries hold egalitarian values, people believe that power is distributed equally. This translates into a powerful middle class, SMEs, a participative and direct communication style, a dislike of control, and leadership is challenged to show expertise. High-power distance countries believe that inequalities are acceptable and that societies should function on hierarchies. The communication style is indirect, people expect to be told what to do and to not show much initiative. Authority and leadership are never challenged.

Power distance also describes the emotional distance between employees and their supervisors. In high-power distance societies employees follow formal rules and procedures and they expect to be given orders. The management style is authoritarian, and the relationships between employees and managers are emotional. In low-power distance societies employees expect to be part of the decision-making process, and relationships between employees and managers are pragmatic. The management style is participative and democratic.

The *uncertainty avoidance* dimension describes how societies deal with ambiguous or unknown situations and how they have created beliefs and institutions to cope with these challenges. Uncertainty avoidance is thus described as the degree to which members of a culture feel threatened by unclear or unknown situations. The need for rules and clear structures is often seen as a measure that is taken to deal with such situations. Especially for trust formation and maintenance between team members, the dimension of uncertainty avoidance is important because trust is about risk taking.

In a society with low uncertainty avoidance, people have a high tolerance for uncertainty and chaos. Uncertainty is considered part of life, and people have learned to live with it and cope without much stress. Therefore, there should not be more rules than necessary. Managers deal with strategic decisions, and the decision process is important, not the details or the content. People are flexible and are used to reacting quickly in changing situations and to taking more risks. Additionally, time functions as a framework for orientation, and it is infinite.

On the other hand, in countries high on uncertainty avoidance everything is planned: from the timetable of the bus or train to the government agenda. There is an emotional need for rules, precision, and formality. People have a hard time tolerating changes and delays and taking risks. Managers deal with operational tasks, and the decision-making details and content are more important than the process. In this society there is a greater predictability of actions and better long-term planning. Time is essential, is finite, and should not be wasted.

The *individualism and collectivism* dimension refers to the extent to which people are integrated into groups and value their own goals over group goals and see themselves as I or we. In individualist societies people take care of themselves and direct family only. Management is about individuals. In collectivist societies people see each other as belonging to several groups that they are loyal to and which take care of them. In a collectivist society, for example, favors are made and one must know certain people and belong to certain groups to receive certain advantages. Management is about groups, and hiring or promoting takes into consideration group membership.

Individualistic societies do business with companies, whereas collectivistic societies attach importance to work with known individuals. In a collectivistic society it is normal to feel and be responsible for even the remotest members of the family. Hence, the group (family, ethnic, organization) is especially important, and loyalty is a key virtue. Loyalty to the group one belongs to is important above all, and everyone takes responsibility for fellow members of their group.

The *masculinity and femininity* dimension is about what predominantly motivates people or what is valued within society – wanting to be the best (masculine) or doing what you like (feminine). A masculine society is driven by competition, achievement, and success – defined as being the best in a field starting in school and continuing in work life. Performance is valued as people often live to work and gives people self-esteem. Managers are competent, assertive, and decisive. The focus is on status. Conflicts are resolved by letting the stronger argument win.

A feminine society values quality of life and caring for others. People value equality, solidarity, and quality at work. Managers strive for consensus; conflicts are resolved by compromise and negotiation. The focus is on well-being rather than status.

Long-term and short-term orientation dimension is about how a society maintains links with its own past and deals with the present and future challenges. Long-term orientation emphasizes thrift, perseverance, adaptation, and persistence to gain future rewards, whereas short-term orientation focuses on fulfilling social obligations and maintaining traditions and norms. Pragmatic societies have a long-term orientation and focus on facts, encouraging thriftiness and perseverance in achieving results. Main work virtues are learning, honesty, responsibility, and self-discipline. Traditional societies have a short-term orientation and are focused on traditions, peer-group pressure on spending and getting things done quickly. Important work virtues are freedom, rights, performance, and independent thinking.

Indulgence and restraint refer to whether people in a society are raised predominantly to try to control their desires and impulses or not. Weak control represents indulgence, strong control is restraint. For a society that values indulgence, leisure time is important. People have a positive attitude towards life, act as they please, and spend money as they wish. A society that values strong control does not emphasize leisure time; they have a pessimist outlook on life and control the gratification of their desires – indulging is wrong. Duty, hard work, and a focus on goals and responsibilities are important.

Cultural dimensions theory has received its share of criticism over the years. Researchers consider it simplistic to conceptualize national culture as homogenous, static, and historically determined (Fougère and Moulettes 2007). What is more, the theory is considered by some as a tool for propagating stereotypes between countries, and the six cultural dimensions are deemed inconsistent and contradictory (McSweeney 2002). The most criticized cultural dimension is masculinity/femininity that researchers criticize as vague, including several femininity types and not being a relevant characteristic of culture – nationality and culture can be characterized in several other ways (Fougère and Moulettes 2007).

Methodologically, the model is criticized for measuring in a quantitative way a complex, unquantifiable construct – culture (Fougère and Moulettes 2007) and for imposing a Western "scientific" viewpoint. Other methodological shortcomings include outdated questionnaires collected in a single multinational organization (McSweeney 2002). Findings from one company across the world cannot be implemented to determine overall cultural dimensions. Criticism has also been pointed that the findings did not provide valid information regarding the culture of the entire country (Ward 2008). With all these shortcomings, cultural dimensions theory remains the most widely recognized and applied theoretical framework in management and organizational studies for the past 40 years (Hofstede, Hofstede, and Minkov 2010).

While acknowledging the limitations of using the country as a proxy for culture, we consider cultural dimensions theory suitable for the purpose of our research to understand cultural preferences and variations in trust practices in Germany and Singapore. We consider this framework a reliable cultural compass that offers a good orientation across multiple cultures rather than a tool that propagates stereotypes.

We argue that the six dimensions are relevant for building and maintaining trust in virtual teams because they pose important questions that can either foster or hinder trust development within remote teams. Since managing expectations has to do with trust, knowing that people from different cultures have different expectations and managing these expectations is essential for trust building.

We acknowledge that every person is different and has a life story that influences socialization and cultural values. While people do not fall into one or the other dimension because they share nationality, there is a tendency and a preference for certain values rather than others. Additionally, what cultural dimensions theory emphasizes is that these dimensions and the scores that each country has on the scale are dependent on the other countries.

> The replication studies correlating the old country scores with related variables available on a year-by-year basis in many cases find no weakening of the correlations. A good reason for this is that the country scores on the dimensions do not provide absolute country positions, but only their positions relative to the other countries in the set.
>
> (Hofstede 2011)

3.3 Trust practices and culture

Just as anthropologists wondered whether human culture is universal, trust researchers asked whether trust building is universal across cultures or whether people from different cultures build trust differently. Ferrin and Gillespie (2010) addressed this question in their extensive review of quantitative research and concluded that trust is both universal and culture specific. Ferrin and Gillespie found consistent evidence that countries differ in their average level of generalized trust. This difference was correlated with factors such as national wealth, income equality, education, strong formal institutions, and ethnic homogeneity, all of which are largely demographic and geographic. The trustworthiness indicators' ability, benevolence, and integrity (see Chapter 2) are universal but there are also culturally specific components such as thriftiness and respect for authority that appear to be more important in some countries than in others (Dietz, Gillespie, and Chao 2010). Then trust researchers wondered how trust develops in dyadic relations when people from different cultures work together. What they found is that there are universal principles of trust that are manifested and interpreted in culturally specific contexts. In some relationships (e.g., leader-follower, supervisor-subordinate) trust universally mediates relationships across cultural contexts (Wasti, Tan, and Erdil 2011). But in other relationships (e.g., manager and team member citizenship behavior) trust is culture specific (Henderson 2005). For example, management consultants must reconcile the values of their own organization with their clients' expectations driven by the need to build a positive client relationship while keeping their own organization's culture (Dietz, Gillespie, and Chao 2010).

A consistent pattern across studies is that while there are universal approaches to building trust, developing context-specific rules is important for building trust across cultures. Cross-cultural trust emerges when project managers and team members look beyond cultural differences and when work on setting up shared rules for their specific work relationships (Möllering and Stache 2007). These rules contribute to a reflexive trust-building process by increasing understanding and predictability between team members.

This is in line with our approach of conceptualizing trust as a social practice (see Chapter 2). Trust exists because of the recurrent, routinized, planned activities performed by virtual team members. Trust in teams has to do with habits or what is understood through routines and practices. When we discuss practices that build trust, we emphasize the idea of creating a common, shared understanding; and when we talk about practices of maintaining trust, the underlying idea is that of acting on behalf of the team, based on these common assumptions. Through repeated positive interaction and sharing of information, trust becomes relatively stable within the team, and interactions must be frequent enough to keep trust going. Maintaining trust means that members of virtual teams work toward keeping trust afloat. They act according to their mutual interests and the rules of their team, and no one takes any action to erode trust.

Creating a shared understanding and acting based on this understanding depend on cultural context and interpretation. In societies where formal hierarchies are valued, people have a different understanding of decision-making than people in more egalitarian, low-power cultures. In one work culture relying on managers and formal rules and procedures is important, and in the other, debates and informal discussions create shared understanding and lead to decisions. Both practices are important in building and maintaining trust depending on the cultural context.

To conclude, theoretical and research evidence demonstrates that trust develops both universally and specifically across cultural contexts. By looking at several remote teams in two different societies, our research aims to understand cultural preferences and variations in trust practices.

3.4 Comparative case studies: trust practices in Germany and Singapore

To understand how remote teams build and maintain trust as a practice, we interviewed team members and project managers working in ten virtual project teams in Germany and Singapore. We asked them about their team experiences, the activities they engage in to build trust, the activities they describe as maintaining trust as well as the challenges they faced as a virtual team (see Appendix 2. Interview guide).

We selected Germany and Singapore for our case studies because both countries are successful economies in the world; Singapore is the second most competitive economy among 140 economies, and Germany ranks as the third most competitive economy (World Economic Forum 2019). While both societies are examples of economic success, they have different value systems, do business, and build trust and teamwork differently. Germany, a Western European culture is characterized by low power distance, individualism, masculinity, high uncertainty avoidance, long-term orientation, and restraint. Singapore, a South East Asian culture emphasizes high power distance, high collectivism, femininity, low uncertainty avoidance, long-term orientation, and indulgence. And because they vary on cultural values, we wanted to explore how these differences relate to trust practices in virtual project teams.

We wanted to have rich and varied information, so fieldwork accessibility and convenience determined our case selection (see Appendix 3. Description of case studies). Together with two independent coders, we coded and analyzed the data using qualitative content analysis and developed a taxonomy of trust practices. Our coding framework captures ten categories of trust practices that emerged from the data. In each category we find cultural preferences and variations that we present in Figure 3.1 and discuss in the following.

In virtual teams, members emphasize the need for trust building at the beginning of their interactions, in the project initiation phase – "we have to set the stage for trust, we create the conditions needed, we have some tools that enable us to build trust" (RKIW11). In the beginning of their interactions, teams describe that they create rules of communication, share personal information, and develop common goals and expectations to build trust.

Because remote teams rely only on mediated communication to work together, they emphasize that agreeing upon and implementing rules are a priority from the beginning of the project. Trust is built because team members develop rules and structures to handle information complexity and frequently interact to structure the content, frequency, and channels of communication.

Remote teams develop rules regarding communication content, so that team members receive the relevant information that concerns them and their tasks. This is an important aspect of the

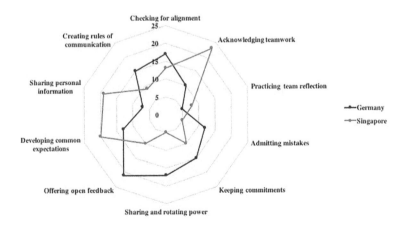

Figure 3.1 Trust Building and Maintaining Practices in Germany and Singapore.

practice of building trust; once this practice exists, team members act on behalf of each other, based on trust, on the assumption that they know which information the other team members need. Team members decide for each other which information is relevant and irrelevant and for whom. So, to manage information flow, they only send emails to team members who benefit from that information. The other team members depend on the information shared to progress on their work so if one team member thinks some information is not relevant for another team member this can have important consequences for the team.

> If we send the message to one person in the team, then we don't put everybody in copy. On the other hand, if we know that in the long run somebody else is going to benefit from that information, we put that person in the copy, but in the subject line we characterize exactly what we expect because of this email.
>
> (SBIW4)

Not sharing confidential and sensitive information outside of the team becomes a practice of building trust: for example, sharing confidential information about competitors or adopting unethical strategies. "A strategy that I know from one of our competitors, is to make them believe that is reality, when in fact it's not" (AKIW2). This is interpreted as a trust-building practice because of the implicit assumption that sensitive information will not be shared outside of the team. Not betraying the team by sharing confidential information that, if distributed outside, would become a competitive advantage for other teams. This is an essential action for trust because it means acting according to their mutual interest as a team and the rules of communication that have been developed.

Rules about frequency of communication build trust in teams. On the one hand, rules for communication need to emphasize regular and predictable communication, and, on the other hand, communication should be kept flexible. "It's important to get into a rhythm with the team, we do that when we interact frequently via multiple channels" (DZIW6). For example, daily standups or weekly meetings occur regularly and predictably but if something unplanned happens each team member can organize an ad hoc meeting. "Please if something urgent pops up do not wait, call or send me an instant message on the app. We don't wait until the next meeting..." (RWIW13).

Rules about which communication channel (i.e., email, chat, video, phone) to use for which information are important to build trust in the team.

> For example, which communication tool for which purpose? If we want to get immediate feedback, we do not use email, we call. (...) Or for example, if we do not understand a communication in an email, we immediately write that.
>
> (SBIW4)

When information is ambiguous, incomplete, or sensitive, or if it requires an immediate response, then calling is better than writing an email because it allows team members to make sense of the situation and construct meaning together.

> For example, too many emails, too much email ping-pong... Always the managers in copy, yeah? So, we need a different way of dealing with information. We came up with a couple of ideas like instead of sending an email we call each other, we chat online... More direct communication instead of email.
>
> (AKIW2)

And then what becomes relevant is which type of information to share (i.e., discerning between relevant and irrelevant information, between sensitive information that cannot be shared outside the team, and between information that can be shared with other departments and stakeholders), and using which channel. Written communication is the preferred way of communication: "In our virtual team we prefer emails because it's easier to track, stays on the server, you can always have a back-up of what has happened, who agreed on what and when" (KBIW10). Not betraying the team by sharing confidential information that, if distributed outside, would become a competitive advantage for other teams.

While in both cultures creating rules of communication is important for virtual teams, there are some nuances in how this practice is described and used. An explanation for this is the uncertainty avoidance dimension that translates into a strong emphasis on structure, details, and clarity in Germany. In Singapore, a low uncertainty avoidance culture, we see a preference for keeping communication more flexible and continuous through phone updates backed-up by written reports.

So, first we have a spontaneous Skype call and then we send the email, but you know just to make sense of the requirement and task, I mean sure we have meetings but sometimes we just need to be in touch.

(IVIW12)

Sharing personal information is another important practice of building trust in virtual teams. Because virtual teams do not have the time or space to get to know each other like collocated teams do, they describe how they actively work on this. They describe how informal chatting creates opportunities to increase perceived similarity and familiarity between team members while decreasing perceptions of dissimilarity and distance (e.g., virtual coffee breaks, WhatsApp Group/Slack). "We decided to make a WhatsApp group where everyone shared some funny pictures of their pets or of what they cooked during the weekend. Like a virtual coffee break, you know?" (IVIW12). Another example is offering each team member opportunities to share personal information at the beginning of each virtual meeting to understand their personal context, their different workload and availability.

Taking time at the beginning of the meeting to ask: How was your weekend? What is the weather like? How are your kids? Something small like that has a huge impact on trust, it brings us closer as a team.

(AKIW2)

Another tool is organizing remote team hangouts where they can interact and get to know each other besides work (e.g., a virtual coffee break, pizza for everyone in the team, fun Friday).

In both Germany and Singapore, sharing personal information is important for building trust in virtual teams. There are some variations that can be explained through the individualism/collectivism dimension. In Germany, sharing personal information is usually considered useful at the beginning of the meeting, and it focuses on individual hobbies and interests. In Singapore, a collectivist society, the emphasis is on sharing personal information about family and friends.

Another important practice of building trust is offering open feedback. Especially in virtual teams where the project manager is not conveniently located next door and you cannot talk whenever you like, giving each other open feedback is essential. Team members act on the assumption that their feedback will be interpreted positively, and this produces trust

> We say what we think and then we do what we say yeah? Trust is more visible in how team members give each other feedback. Are they able and are they willing to give each other open feedback? If yes, that is already part of trust, yeah? We trust each other and we are able to give each other feedback: we really say what we're thinking, yeah?.
>
> (AKIW2)

Team members are encouraged to speak up and voice their concerns.

> The idea is that people say what they need, they speak up. If they do not because we're in this virtual kind of environment or whatever you have to call them out during the meeting. Like saying "Look, you have to be reasonable: this is what this person needs, this is what that person needs."
>
> (MNIW9)

While this practice is described in all case studies, there are differences. In Germany direct and blunt feedback builds and maintains trust, it is valued and considered stimulating to move the project forward. In Singapore consensus builds and maintains trust, the more team members agree on what must be done, the more the project will move forward.

In line with the practice of offering open feedback, it is acknowledging team members' work as a team practice that maintains trust. This means recognizing the work that team members have made, and it is important to do this with all group members or important project stakeholders. There are several actions such as sending an email with the project owners copied, thanking each team member for the tasks completed and the deadlines reached. These activities are done at the beginning of virtual meetings.

Sharing and rotating power describes the trust-building practice in which project and performance expectations are clearly established and team members are encouraged to speak up and participate in decision-making. Especially in virtual teams it is motivating for team members to have control over their work: "We defined what we needed to do, and we put the expectations very clearly, and then everyone just took charge, and we did what we had to do. Like everyone has control over what they do" (RKIW11). Empowering the team means giving team members the chance to take responsibility over what they do. Micromanaging does the opposite; it gives team members the feeling that they have no control and no decision regarding their work.

In both Germany and Singapore sharing power is described as building trust, but there are differences in the meaning of this practice. In Germany, a low-power distance society, this translates into the belief that managers and team members are equals and everyone expects to be consulted on team-related topics. In Singapore, a high-power distance society, team members respect management and expect to be told what to do. Here team members must be actively supported and encouraged to speak up and participate in decisions.

Team trust is maintained by keeping commitments and delivering on target, following through on promises

> Then they mention a lot that happens when people listen to each other, asking questions, being curious about each other. But also showing they have some commitment, like 'Ok, we said that we will do this, and I did it or I took it seriously – what we talked about the last time. That also builds trust.
>
> (KWIW10)

This practice is valued in the same way in both cultures. It seems that keeping commitments is considered an important practice for maintaining trust, and when this does not happen trust may become problematic and conflicts may appear.

When conflicts are managed in a productive, constructive manner this maintains trust by allowing a good flow of information and by developing a shared understanding of what is happening within the team.

> There are times where we've had to take time-out in meetings and just try to make sense of what was happening. If we are having problems delivering on what we agreed, we need to get to the real issue: we cannot fulfill the requests or we are not clear on what we are being asked for. Starting to get to the root problem to get to why there is a misalignment on expectations. So, it is kind of like staying true to the team, keep trust going.
>
> (DZIW6)

Germany is a low power society; this means that team members speak up and challenge management. Disagreement is expected, and team members are encouraged to voice their opinions and challenge management, thus showing their competence and skills. Team members have high autonomy, and the manager is expected to perform minimum control over team members' work. But in Singapore, a high-power distance country, one does not simply disagree and challenge leadership. Humiliation and embarrassment are to be avoided to maintain reputation in front of peers. One on one discussions are preferred when disagreements exist, but achievements must be recognized in front of the whole team and attributed to the whole group.

The practice of admitting weaknesses and the fact that the team accepts them, enacting and perpetuating this, are distinctive to trust. Consequently, the virtual team starts acting as a safe environment for team members to ask questions, voice their opinion, and present even their more controversial ideas. Additionally, it allows the team to accept the mistakes that others have made because "we are all human beings" and to reflect on their team strengths and weaknesses.

> It was very awkward that it happened, but that is also okay, because we are all human beings, we sometimes act irrational, and it has to do with trust that this can be mended. And then how do you start getting back to normal shape? Somebody does the first step, sending an email: 'Are you okay? Shall we talk about it again? Maybe just you and me...
>
> (FKIW1)

Showing vulnerability, i.e., "personal sides of yourself that are not so polished" (FHIW1) are also important to trust building because they signal to others that you are interested in the team and you are willing to put in yourself, your time, and your effort for the benefit of the team.

Practicing team reflection maintains trust. Examples of team reflection activities described are celebrating team milestones, taking time-out, and performing lessons learned. A lessons-learned session means discussing the challenges that team members face, why some tasks have been carried out in a certain way, and developing strategies to improve teamwork. Lessons learned usually occur upon task-completion and toward the end of a project phase. The term refers to maintaining trust because it means reflecting on the team's progress and making sense of team events such as conflicts, team decisions, and misunderstandings. Allowing for team time-out means acting based on trust by reflecting on what has been achieved, what went well, and what did not.

> We put more focus on the process as such and talk with the team about it and just have some meta-reflection about it, like 'Ok, we worked on these tasks. How did it work? And how can we just... What has been good and what do we need to strengthen or...yeah?' That is a good time-out for the group to think about what we have achieved, what mistakes we made and why.
>
> (KBW10)

Another tool is celebrating the team's success, a practice of maintaining trust both between manager and team members and between members.

> When we reach a milestone or achieve a target, we just celebrate that in the project team. So, we say within the project team 'Ok, we have really succeeded in implementing a system that is so easy that the people can... like to use it and feel like they can also influence it still.' We can participate in developing it.
>
> (KBW10)

Because of project complexity and duration, checking for alignment in virtual teams is not only expected but also required, thus building and maintaining trust. Checking for common understanding and alignment are practices of maintaining trust, as they refer to asking questions about the understanding of the project requirements, clarifying roles and responsibilities, and monitoring each other so that the team completes the agreed-upon tasks. These activities maintain trust because the remote team members act based on the assumption that control is part of their tasks, and they decide which tasks require control and when. "To keep trust we want to resolve these differences: clear channels of communication, everyone aligned to the same goals, and a sufficient but not excessive amount of control in place" (RWIW13). In this sense, monitoring becomes part of the team's task to complete a high-quality project on time and within budget.

> Control cannot be delegated. We are all responsible. Yes, the task is so complex that we need to plan, structure, and report.

We need to break down the specific content that is in the software: project management activities, what we did so far in terms of risk management, stakeholder management and risk analysis, what you do, your deliveries are the content, the daily business. Our responsibility is to manage the deliverables, to check that complex tasks are completed on time, and to keep track of the project flow.

(PMIW16)

It became clear that without this tool, the process of monitoring becomes an almost impossible task, since the project is overly complex.

In both cultures checking for alignment is mentioned as a practice that maintains trust but there are some variations. Scoring high on uncertainty avoidance, in Germany people have an indisputable preference for control. Details are important and create certainty that a certain task or project has been thoroughly analyzed and monitored. In Singapore – the lowest ranked country on the uncertainty avoidance dimension – this means that people are willing to accept that not everything can be controlled and that they focus on monitoring the process, rather than the details.

In conclusion, we find that remote teams in both Germany and Singapore describe the same type of practices that build and maintain trust (e.g., creating rules of communication, sharing personal information, keeping commitments) but with some variations in meanings and interpretations. In Germany, virtual teams describe that competence is important in building and maintaining trust within the team. Team members and managers are equals, and team members challenge leadership to show competence and build trust. Communication is direct and blunt, team members build trust by committing to tell each other the truth, and give open and honest feedback – everyone is responsible for their own performance. The responsibility is divided between team members and managers. Details are important and create certainty that tasks or projects have been thoroughly analyzed. Team members are used to having everything planned in detail and need more time to embrace changes. Time is spent at the beginning of the project to discuss and carefully plan everything in detail.

Virtual teams in Singapore describe that to successfully build and maintain trust there needs to be relationship harmony between team members, and the project manager is considered key in maintaining good relationships within the team. Also, the project manager is expected to carry the responsibility for the team and provide clear directions that team members follow without much questioning. Communication is indirect and subtle, team members build trust by striving for consensus and balance, every team member feels respected by the others, especially more experienced, older team members should not be disagreed with in front of the team, but rather one on one or in front of the project manager. Team members are willing to accept ambiguity and uncertainty and are flexible with rules.

In the next chapter, we discuss the theoretical and practical implications of our findings as well as future research directions.

References

Chanlat, J-F. 2012. "Anthropologie Des Organisations." In *Encyclopédie des Ressources Humaines*, edited by J. Allouche, 23–42. Paris: Buibert.

———. 2017. "Management, Diversity, Equal Opportunity, and Social Cohesion in France: The Republic Resistant to Differences." In *Management and Diversity*, edited by M. Ozbilgin and J. F. Chanlat, 112–35. Bingley: Emerald Group Publishing.

Dietz, G., N. Gillespie, and G. T. Chao. 2010. "Unravelling the Complexities of Trust and Culture." *Organizational Trust: A Cultural Perspective* 1: 3–41.

Ferrin, D. L., and N. Gillespie. 2010. "Trust Differences across National-Societal Cultures: Much to Do, or Much Ado about Nothing." *Organizational Trust: A Cultural Perspective* 1: 42–86.

Fougère, M., and A. Moulettes. 2007. "The Construction of the Modern West and the Backward Rest: Studying the Discourse of Hofstede's Culture's Consequences." *Journal of Multicultural Discourses* 2 (1): 1–19.

Geertz, C. 1973. *The Interpretation of Cultures*. Vol. 5019. New York: Basic Books.

Henderson, J. K. 2005. "Language Diversity in International Management Teams." *International Studies of Management & Organization* 35 (1): 66–82.

Hofstede, G. 1980. *Culture's Consequences: International Differences in Work-Related Values*. Beverly Hills, CA: Sage.

Hofstede, G. 2001. *Culture's Consequences: Comparing Values, Behaviors, Institutions and Organizations across Nations*. 2nd ed. Thousand Oaks, CA: Sage Publications.

Hofstede, G. 2011. "Dimensionalizing Cultures: The Hofstede Model in Context." *Online Readings in Psychology and Culture* 2 (1): 919–2307.

Hofstede, G., and M. H. Bond. 1988. "The Confucius Connection: From Cultural Roots to Economic Growth." *Organizational Dynamics* 16 (4): 5–21.

Hofstede, G., G. J. Hofstede, and M. Minkov. 2010. *Cultures and Organizations: Software of the Mind Intercultural Cooperation and Its Important for Survival*. 3rd ed. London: McGraw-Hill Education.

McSweeney, B. 2002. "Hofstede's Model of National Cultural Differences and Their Consequences: A Triumph of Faith-a Failure of Analysis." *Human Relations* 55 (1): 89–118.

Möllering, G., and F. Stache. 2007. "German-Ukrainian Business Relationships: Trust Development in the Face of Institutional Uncertainty and Cultural Differences." MPIfG Discussion Paper, No 7/11

Schein, E. H. 2010. *Organizational Culture and Leadership*. Vol. 2. San Francisco, CA: John Wiley & Sons.

Schwartz, S. H. 2012. "An Overview of the Schwartz Theory of Basic Values." *Online Readings in Psychology and Culture* 2 (1): 919–2307.

Staples, D. S., and L. Zhao. 2006. "The Effects of Cultural Diversity in Virtual Teams versus Face-to-Face Teams." *Group Decision and Negotiation* 15 (4): 389–406.

Triandis, H. C. 1972. *The Analysis of Subjective Culture*. 1st ed. New York: Wiley-IEEE Press.

Ward, C. 2008. "Thinking Outside the Berry Boxes: New Perspectives on Identity, Acculturation and Intercultural Relations." *International Journal of Intercultural Relations* 32 (2): 105–14.

Wasti, S. A., H. H. Tan, and S. E. Erdil. 2011. "Antecedents of Trust across Foci: A Comparative Study of Turkey and China." *Management and Organization Review* 7 (2): 279–302.

Wilkinson, R & Bevir, M (ed.) (2019). The World Economic Forum. In *The Encyclopedia of Governance*. Sage Publications Ltd.

4 Discussion

4.1 Research summary

This book looks at building and maintaining trust as social practices. It focuses on the actions and interactions of team members and managers working in virtual teams in their real-life work context. Our research proposes a new conceptualization of trust as a social practice, for which the unit of analysis is the practice (see Section 2.3). Moving beyond shared beliefs of trustworthiness between team members and collective sets of expectations to trust practices, as actions and interactions between team members, allows exploration of a comprehensive, holistic view of trust.

We proposed a model to analyze trust as a practice focusing on the processes that occur at team level (e.g., signaling, interpreting, negotiating, and cooperating), and we illustrated this model with empirical evidence from three interactions between remote team members and managers: producing new rules of communication, developing a client management strategy, and adjusting the reporting tool. The first interaction illustrates how a remote team engages in new rules of communication by changing the organizational practices of writing long emails and developing strategies to manage relevant and irrelevant information. The second interaction shows how the team discusses and produces a new strategy to handle client expectations, and the third interaction demonstrates how the team adapts the organizational reporting tool and changes it to fit its functionalities and project requirements (see Section 2.5).

We then explored the practices that build and maintain trust (e.g., creating rules of communication, sharing personal information, keeping commitments), discussing the cultural variations in Germany and Singapore (see Section 3.4). In Germany, for example, team members build trust by committing to tell each other the truth regardless of possible conflicts, while in Singapore trust

DOI: 10.4324/9781003095781-4

is built by striving for consensus and balance, and team members should not be openly disagreed with in front of the team. Additionally, in Singapore the project manager is considered essential in maintaining trust and good relationships within the team. Another trust practice mentioned in both cultures is creating rules for communication. In Germany, rules and details are important and create certainty that tasks or projects have been thoroughly analyzed, while in Singapore team members are willing to accept ambiguity and uncertainty and are flexible with rules.

Our findings contribute theoretically to the trust and cross-cultural management literature and practically to organizational interventions and team training effectiveness.

4.2 Theoretical contribution

Our research demonstrates a new theoretical approach for conceptualizing and operationalizing trust in remote teams, from a practice perspective, and illustrates this empirically. By observing and analyzing team interactions, we discover how a remote team produces and reproduces trust through signaling, interpreting, negotiating, and cooperating. Also, we explore the different practices that build and maintain trust (e.g., creating rules of communication, sharing, and rotating power, and checking for common understanding) in two cultural contexts, in Germany and Singapore.

So, what do we know now that we did not know before? How does our research affect the way we conceptualize trust building in remote teams across cultures – and possibly beyond? First, this study affects the way building and maintaining trust in remote teams and in teams in general are conceptualized and operationalized, because it explains how trust develops in team interactions rather than shared beliefs or collective sets of expectations (models which we described in Chapter 2, Sections 2.2 and 2.3). Second, we illustrate the different trust practices that remote teams use along with cultural preferences and variations. While there are universal approaches to building trust, developing context-specific rules is important for building trust across cultures (demonstrated in Chapter 3, Section 3.4).

Why is a practice perspective on trust in teams a good alternative to shared beliefs of trustworthiness or collective sets of expectations? Looking at trust from a practice perspective reveals more than can be discovered by studying shared beliefs and collective expectations. A practice perspective offers a framework that incorporates the actions, interactions, and structures in which remote teams are embedded (which we proposed in Chapter 3). This approach is worthwhile because it focuses on patterns of meaningful activities that build and maintain trust. Our contribution thus moves current research from demonstrating that trust is important in challenging and uncertain contexts, to the path of how trust becomes important by meaning and interpretation (i.e., signaling, interpreting, negotiating, and cooperating).

Previous studies show that frequent interaction and information sharing build and maintain trust in teams (Wilson, Straus, and McEvily 2006; Fulmer and Gelfand 2012). But for remote teams, it is vital to establish norms and routines about information content (relevant and irrelevant information, sensitive information that cannot be shared outside the team, and information that can be shared with other departments and with stakeholders); information frequency (positive and negative nonverbal signals); and information channel (email, chat, face-to-face, phone). The literature is substantial on trust and control (Möllering 2005; Fuglsang and Jagd 2015), yet the practice of checking for alignment that we describe goes further, because it explores their complementary relationship and the importance of the meaning that team members give to their interactions.

What is more, our study incorporates views from two different cultural contexts – Germany and Singapore. Our research illustrates the nuances of building and maintaining trust across cultures. While previous research highlighted that trust develops both universally and specifically across cultural contexts (Ferrin and Gillespie 2010), our findings reveal how this happens in practice. The trust practices we identified are mentioned in both cultures, but our analysis goes further to reveal the context-specific preferences and variations.

Additionally, studies on trust in remote teams have been mostly quantitative, but our research makes a qualitative contribution. The chosen field-study approach enabled investigation of the process as it unfolds in the "real-world" context, thus gaining ecological validity.

4.3 Practical implications

Developing trust practices is crucial for organizations that want to maximize the benefits of remote teamwork. As previous research shows, developing and maintaining trust in remote teams is difficult to achieve because of technological complexity, extensive diversity, information ambiguity, and multiple reporting (as we highlight in Section 1.3).

Project managers and team consultants can maximize remote teamwork by developing and fostering trust practices as demonstrated in our study. For instance, in a newly formed remote project, managers and consultants should pay attention to setting up rules and routines from the beginning and be very clear on performance goals and expectations. As the frequency of interaction increases, keeping commitments, sharing, and rotating power, and checking for alignment are practices that maintain trust. Project managers and team consultants can foster team interpretation and meaning making to their tasks, deciding when control is needed and for which tasks or phases of the project.

Also, managers should be aware of cultural preferences and variations to better grasp the patterns of interaction taking place in remote teams. As we demonstrate with data from our case studies, while remote teams in Germany and Singapore describe the same type of practices that build and maintain trust, there are variations in meanings and interpretations that can be crucial for team performance. For example, in both cultures checking for alignment is mentioned as a practice, but in Germany details are important and create certainty that a certain task or project has been analyzed and monitored, while in Singapore the focus is on monitoring the process, rather than the details.

The findings of our research project address some of the issues encountered by team consultants and trainers when designing team interventions and kick-off workshops. First, understanding trust as a social practice emphasizes the idea that exercises and activities must be addressed at the team level. Changing team behavior requires looking at team interactions as repetitive, meaningful, and often unconscious patterns of activities that represent more than the sum of dyadic relations. Second, the description of the trust building and maintaining practices presented in this research project helps consultants and trainers design better kick-off workshops, because they can pay attention exactly to the processes that build and maintain trust (i.e., signaling, interpreting, negotiating, and cooperating) and the cultural preferences and variations.

4.4 Conclusion

The message of this book is that trust is a social practice built and maintained in interaction, in the collective patterns of activities between remote team members and project managers and embedded in organizational tools and national culture. Trust practices are an indicator and an outcome of these activities – relatively stable, agreed-upon, collective patterns of interaction. The findings of this research are important theoretically because they show how trust practices are conceptualized and practiced in remote teams across cultures, and practically because the practices help overcome the challenges of remote teamwork. We hope this book inspires academics and practitioners to use practices as important organizational tools that build and maintain trust across cultures.

References

Ferrin, D. L., and N. Gillespie. 2010. "Trust Differences across National-Societal Cultures: Much to Do, or Much Ado about Nothing." *Organizational Trust: A Cultural Perspective* 1: 42–86.

Fuglsang, L., and S. Jagd. 2015. "Making Sense of Institutional Trust in Organizations: Bridging Institutional Context and Trust." *Organization* 22 (1). https://doi.org/10.1177/1350508413496577.

Fulmer, C. A., and M. J. Gelfand. 2012. "At What Level (and in Whom) We Trust: Trust across Multiple Organizational Levels." *Journal of Management* 38 (4): 1167–1230. https://doi.org/10.1177/0149206312439327.

Möllering, G. 2005. "The Trust/Control Duality: An Integrative Perspective on Positive Expectations of Others." *International Sociology* 20 (3): 283–305. https://doi.org/10.1177/0268580905055478.

Wilson, J. M., S. G. Straus, and B. McEvily. 2006. "All in Due Time: The Development of Trust in Computer-Mediated and Face-to-Face Teams." *Organizational Behavior and Human Decision Processes* 99 (1): 16–33. https://doi.org/10.1016/j.obhdp.2005.08.001.

Appendix 1
Observation sheet

Online meeting	Focus for observer	What is being observed	Observations
10:00 Welcome (all)	Technology use	Familiar ——— unfamiliar Easy ——— difficult	
	Atmosphere	Open, relaxed ——— closed, tense Formal ——— informal	
	Participants	How many participants? How many departments? Who is not there but was expected to be there? Why?	
10:15 Status update	Team interactions	Who decides, who speaks, and who listens? Who is speaking first from the participants? Who is speaking/listening more? Do participants stick to the meeting agenda, or are they negotiating some parts? Are they curious about each other? Are they paying attention?	
	Team communication	What do they choose to present about themselves – role, function, performance, or something personal? How do they talk about their project expectations and their functional role? How do they negotiate their project objectives?	

(*Continued*)

Online meeting	Focus for observer	What is being observed	Observations
10:30 Project planning presentation (KR)	Team communication	How is the project manager communicating to the team members? Who is the customer/company expectations for this project? Is there a history of working together? What are the project objectives as communicated by stakeholders? What is the status? What are the major challenges and risks of this project? How are they communicating? What information are they sharing? Personal/ professional?	
10:40 Project planning discussion (team)	Team interactions	How are they building their reputations and roles within the team? Is everyone participating? Who speaks the most? Who listens the most?	

Appendix 2
Interview guide

Interview questions	Follow-up questions
1 What brought you to work in this field?	1.1 What does your work involve?
	1.2 What aspects of your work do you like?
2 How would you describe a team you have worked with that you are proud of?	2.1 How would you describe a successful team? What about an unsuccessful team? In your opinion what role (if any) does trust play?
	2.2 Can you tell me more about trust in teams, and what does it mean to you?
	2.3 How do you recognize trust in teams?
Context	
3 Let us go back to the team you are proud of and talk about the organization that team was working for and your role	3.1 Type of industry (production/consultancy/government)
	3.2 Values of the organization (competitive/collaborative culture)
	3.3 Private/family/government owned
	3.4 What was your role? What did you have to do for that team?
4 Now I would like to discuss with you the specifics of that team, could you tell me more about...?	4.1 Team structure and roles
	a Team composition: number of members, background, culture, expertise, gender
	b Type of team: permanent/temporary; hybrid/virtual; self-directed/managed
	c Team structure: formal/informal; self-directed/formal leader; was the team leader formally assigned or did she emerge as one?
	d Team dynamics and roles: clear/unclear roles assigned by the team leader
	4.2 Overall purpose of the team
	a Organizational change (merger, acquisition, downsizing, outsourcing) or innovation (new product development)
	b Task complexity, interdependence

(Continued)

Interview questions	*Follow-up questions*

Trust building

5 How did that team start off?

5.1 How was everyone introduced?
5.2 Was everyone enthusiastic about working in that team/project?
5.3 How frequent were the interactions within the team (meetings, calls, emails)?

6 How were the initial interactions within that team?

6.1 How did everyone share information?
6.2 Did everyone know who was doing what?
6.3 Was it clear what was expected from the team?
6.5 Were there any perceived risks in the beginning? Did trust play a role?

7 How did that team further develop?

7.1 How did the team organize regular check-ups?
7.2 How was the team performance evaluated?
7.3 How were decisions taken in that team?
7.4 What role do you think trust had?

8 Was there a turning point in the development of that team?

8.1 Team coordination: Was it easy for the team members to coordinate? Thug of war: Were some members pulling against other members? Why (not)?
8.2 Team motivation: Was everyone committed to the tasks and the overall goal of the team? Why (not)?
8.3 Conflict management: Can you tell me about a time when there was a conflict within this team? How did this conflict impact the team?

Reflections

9 How do you feel about your experience working with that team?

9.1 What did you learn from working with that team?
9.2 How would you evaluate that team in terms of performance?

10 Any suggestions?

Is there anything that you would like to add that you think is important for trust in teams?

Appendix 3
Case studies

No.	Code	Project	Team members	Company
1	AKCS2	Virtual new product development team in Germany client external project	Eleven members in Germany, Morocco, and Romania	Large automotive spare-parts producer
2	SBCS3	Customized IT solution to client external project	Six members in Germany and Japan	Large IT solutions developer
3	DRCS4	Communication strategy development and implementation internal	Seven members spread across Germany	Large multinational communication
4	YFCS5	Organizational transformation project client external	Five members in Singapore and Switzerland	Large consumer goods producer
5	DZCS6	Virtual sales project team internal	Four members in Singapore and the US	Medium-sized social media consulting company
6	WLCS8	Employer branding strategy internal strategic project	Five members in Singapore and China	Large consumer goods transporter logistics
7	KBCS10	Knowledge-management system internal strategic project	Twelve members in Germany and Sweden	Large non-profit organization
8	IVCS12	Database training program internal strategic	Seven members in Germany, Slovakia, and Romania	Medium-sized HR consulting company

(*Continued*)

No.	*Code*	*Project*	*Team members*	*Company*
9	RWSC13	Scrum development and implementation project external	Five members in Germany and Romania	Large E-commerce company
10	MLCS15	Operational application development internal project	Ten members in Singapore, Hong Kong, and Germany	Medium-sized certification company

Index

anthropology 39
assistant project manager
  28, 31

benevolence 15, 16, 40, 45
building and maintaining
  trust 14–36, 45, 47, 55, 56,
  59–61
case studies 69–70
client expectations 3, 29, 32, 33,
  36, 59
Cohen, S. G. 4
collectivism 43
communication 2, 3, 5, 14, 15, 29,
  31, 48–50, 55–7, 59, 60; rules of
  29–30
complexity 4, 5, 6, 10, 27, 36, 48,
  55, 61
cooperation/cooperating process 26,
  30, 31, 33, 35
cost efficiency 4
criticism 44
cross-cultural trust 46
cultures 3, 4, 6–7, 39–48, 50–3, 56,
  60, 61, 63; cultural differences 40,
  46; cultural dimensions theory
  3, 40–5; cultural values 36, 40,
  45, 47; defining 39–40; in remote
  project teams 39–57

Davis, J. H. 15
diversity 3–7, 61
dyadic interactions 26, 27

Ehnert, I. 25
emails 6, 28, 30, 31, 49–52, 54, 61
extensive diversity 6

femininity 43
Ferrin, D. L. 45
frequent interaction 15, 17, 61

Germany 28, 40, 45, 47–57,
  59–60, 62
Gersick, C. J. G. 9
Gibson, C. B. 4
Gillespie, N. 45
Gully, S. M. 10

Hofstede, G. 41
human culture 39, 45

individualistic societies 43
indulgence 44
information ambiguity 7
information systems 1, 14
innovation 4
integrity 15, 16, 45
intercultural management 3, 39
interdependence 1
interpersonal trust 14–15
interpreting process 26, 33, 35
interview guide 67–8

Kluckhohn 41
Kozlowski, S. W. 10
Kramer, R. M. 17–19
Kroeber 41

long-term orientation 43, 47

Marks, M. A. 10
masculinity 43
Mathieu, J. E. 10
Mayer, R. C. 15
Meyerson, D. 17, 19
Möllering, G. 24, 25
Monteiro, P. 21, 22
multidimensional psychological
    construct 15
multiple reporting relationships 8

Nason, E. R. 10
national culture 39–41, 44, 63
negotiation/negotiating process 26,
    30, 31, 33, 35
Nicolini, D. 21–2

observation sheet 65–6
organizational behavior 20
organizational culture 39–40
organizational processes 1, 20–2, 41
organizational rules 15, 18, 26
organizational system 18, 20, 21,
    23, 24
organizational trust 14–15

performance and organizational
    learning 4
power distance 41, 42
practice approaches 19–22
practice perspective 2, 3, 19, 21, 23,
    27, 60
professional roles 18
project management tool 24, 35, 36
project managers 8, 17–19, 27,
    28, 30, 31, 33–5, 46, 47, 56, 62;
    trust 18
project teams 1, 2, 9, 14–24, 47

reflexive trust-building process 46
remote development team: building
    and maintaining trust in 27–36
remote project teams 1, 39–57
remote teams 1–9, 19, 28, 47, 48,
    60–2; building and maintaining
    trust in 14–36; characteristics and
    challenges of 3–8; development
    of 8–11; members 6, 11, 59, 63

remote teamwork 1, 61–3
reporting tool 34
restraint 44
risk 1, 4, 5, 8, 11, 17, 31, 33

Schatzki, T. R. 21
Schoorman, F. D. 15
sharing personal information 51,
    56, 59
short-term orientation 43
signaling 25, 26, 33
Singapore 36, 40, 45, 47–57, 59–62
Singapore trust 59
Smith, E. M. 10
stakeholder risk analysis 8
subcultures 40
swift trust model 17–20

team 7, 9, 10, 14, 18, 26–31, 33–5,
    46, 49, 50, 53, 54, 60; case
    study 27–36; communication
    19, 24; culture 39–40; decision
    process 26; decisions 31, 34, 55;
    interactions 2, 3, 19, 25, 29, 31,
    34–6, 60, 62; performance 20,
    21, 62; practices 23, 24, 52; trust
    14–15, 19, 23, 53
team development 7, 9, 10; models
    of 9, 10
teamwork 40, 47, 54
technological complexity 5
temporary team 17, 18
time allocation diversity 6
trust 1–3, 14, 15, 17–19, 23, 24,
    26–9, 36, 45–7, 60, 61; behavior
    15; building and maintaining
    14–36; comparative case
    studies 47–57; defining 14–15;
    developing 7, 8; development 1,
    9, 17, 19, 25; in Germany and
    Singapore 47–57; impressions
    19; integrative model of 15–17;
    novel approach 20–7; practical
    implications 61–2; practices 2, 3,
    23–7, 36, 45–8, 59–63; practice
    theories, organizational research
    20–3; in remote project teams
    39–57; researchers 45, 46; as
    social practice 20–7; theoretical
    contribution 60–1

trustors 15–18
trustworthiness 2, 16–18, 27, 59, 60; shared beliefs of 2, 27, 59, 60
trustworthiness indicators 16, 45

uncertainty 1; avoidance 41, 42, 56; avoidance dimension 42
universal human culture 39

values 40
variations 2, 3, 40, 45, 47, 48, 51, 56, 60–2

virtual team members 40, 46
virtual teams 2, 3, 7, 8, 26, 27, 36, 45, 46, 48, 50–2, 55, 56; *see also individual entries*

Weick, K. E. 17, 19
work culture 47
workshops 3, 62
Wright, A. 25

Zaccaro, S. J. 10

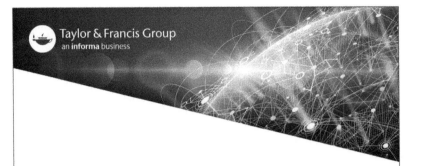